The Complete Ketogenic Instant Pot Mini Cookbook

Quick, Healthy, and Foolproof Instant Pot Keto Recipes for Rapid Weight Loss & Saving Time using 3-Quart Models

Copyright © 2018 by Sarah Orwell –
All Rights Reserved

No part of this publication may be reproduced, stored in a retrieval system, or transmitted in any form or by any means, electronic, mechanical, photocopying, recording, scanning or otherwise, except as permitted under Sections 107 or 108 of the 1976 United States Copyright Act, without the prior written permission of the Publisher, except for the inclusion of brief quotations in a review.

<u>Disclaimer and Terms of Use</u>
The Author and Publisher has strived to be as accurate and complete as possible in the creation of the book, notwithstanding the fact that she does not warrant or represent at any time that the contents within are accurate due to rapidly changing nature of the Internet. While all attempts have been made to verify information provided in this publication, the Author and Publisher assumes no responsibility for errors, omissions, or contrary interpretation of the subject matter herein. Any perceived slights of specific persons, peoples, or organizations are unintentional. In practical advice books, like anything else in life, there are no guarantees of results. Readers are cautioned to rely on their own judgement about their individual circumstances and act accordingly. This book is not intended for use as a source of legal, medical, business, accounting or financial advice. All readers are advised to seek services of competent professionals in the legal, medical, business, accounting, and finance fields.

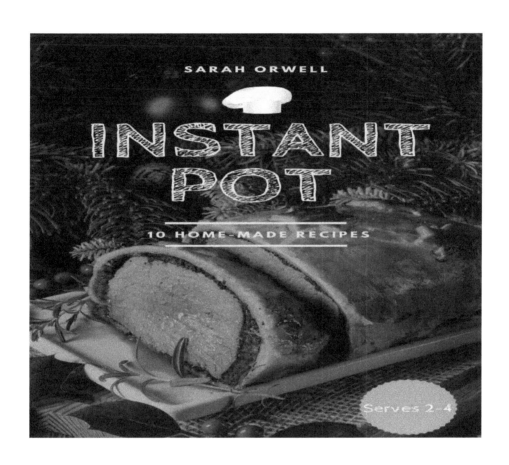

Free Instant Pot Home-Made Recipes For You

✓ easy to make

✓ includes images

✓ cosmicrecipes.com/tasteofpot

Table of Contents

Introduction 8
    The Instant Pot Mini 8
    Getting to Know Your Instant Pot Mini 9
    What To Do Before Your First Use 10
    Understanding the Buttons of the Instant Pot Mini 11
    Why You Need an Instant Pot Mini in Your Home? 13
    Pressure Release Methods 14
    The Ketogenic Diet: The Basics 15
    Defining the Ketogenic Diet 16
    How Does the Ketogenic Diet Work? 16
    Foods You Can Eat on a Ketogenic Diet 17
    Foods to Avoid on a Ketogenic Diet 19
    Safety Considerations & Possible Side Effects of the Keto Diet 20

My Cooking Tips 22

14-Day Meal Plan 23
    Day 1 - Monday 23
    Day 2 - Tuesday 23
    Day 3 - Wednesday 23
    Day 4 - Thursday 23
    Day 5 - Friday 23
    Day 6 - Saturday 24
    Day 7 - Sunday 24
    Day 8 - Monday 24
    Day 9 - Tuesday 24
    Day 10 - Wednesday. 24
    Day 11 - Thursday 24

Day 12 - Friday 25
Day 13 - Saturday 25
Day 14 - Sunday 25

Instant Pot Mini Breakfast Recipes 26

1. Keto Friendly Quiche 26
2. Instant Pot Mini Scotch Eggs 28
3. Instant Pot Mini Hard-Boiled Eggs 30
4. Instant Pot Mini Rice Milk Porridge 31
5. Chocolate Zucchini Muffin Bites 33

Instant Pot Mini Lunch Recipes 35

6. Keto Instant Pot Mini Snow Peas & Bell Pepper 35
7. Instant Pot Mini Spaghetti Squash 37
8. Instant Pot Mini Carnitas Lettuce Wraps 39
9. Instant Pot Mini Ham 41
10. Instant Pot Mini Chili Lime Steak Bowl 43
11. Low-Carb Green Chile Pork Taco Bowl 45
12. Instant Pot Mini Keema 47
13. Instant Pot Mini Pork Carnitas 49
14. Keto Pressure Cooker Garlic Butter Chicken 51

Instant Pot Mini Snack Recipes 53

15. Instant Pot Mini Cauliflower Mash 53
16. Instant Pot Mini Buffalo Ranch Chicken with Dip 55
17. Smokey Barbecue Beans 57
18. Brussels Sprouts 59
19. Prosciutto-wrapped Asparagus Canes 61
20. Steamed Artichokes 63
21. Instant Pot Mini Cottage Cheese 65

Instant Pot Mini Dinner Recipes 67

22. Curried Chicken with Cauliflower 67

23.	Instant Pot Mini Pork Ribs	69
24.	Ropa Vieja	71
25.	Arroz Con Pollo	73
26.	Instant Pot Mini Chicken Curry	75
27.	Shredded Chicken	77
28.	Asian Beef Pot Roast	79
29.	Green Curry Cauliflower & Broccoli	81
30.	Pressure Cooker Pork and Kraut	83
31.	Pork Roast with Mushroom Gravy	85
32.	Belizean Stewed Chicken	87
33.	Dairy Free Beef Stroganoff	89
34.	Keto Instant Pot Mini Mexican Meatloaf	91
35.	Instant Pot Mini No Noodle Lasagna	93
36.	Instant Pot Mini Chicken Tikka Masala	95

Instant Pot Meat & Poultry 97

37.	Holiday Chicken in An Instant Pot Mini	97
38.	Jamaican Jerk Pork Roast	99
39.	Instant Pot Mini Stewed Pork	101
40.	Instant Pot Mini Spare Ribs	103
41.	Mexican Beef	105
42.	Pressure Cooker Pork Chops	107
43.	Balsamic Chicken	109
44.	Pressure Cooker Beef Short Ribs	111
45.	Instant Pot Mini Pork Roast & Gravy	113
46.	Instant Pot Mini Boneless Pork Chops	115
47.	Creamy Salsa Chicken	117

Instant Pot Mini Soups & Stews 119

48.	Instant Pot Mini Chili	119
49.	Low Carb Goulash Soup	121

50.	Cabbage Soup	123
51.	Low-carb Loaded Cauliflower Soup	125
52.	IP Mini Pulled Pork Chili	128
53.	Chickpea Soup	130
54.	Zuppa Toscana	132
55.	Chicken Chili Verde	134
56.	Pressure-Cooked Lamb Stew	136
57.	Spicy Brazilian Fish Stew	138
58.	Chicken Faux Pho	140
59.	Instant Pot Mini Chicken Soup with Kale	142
60.	Beef Brisket Pho	144
61.	Split Asparagus Soup	147
62.	Pork Cheek Stew	149
63.	Quick Onion Soup	151
64.	Instant Pot Mini Beef Curry Stew	153
65.	Low Carb Bone Broth	155
66.	Tomatillo Chili	157
67.	Broccoli Cheese Soup	159

Instant Pot Dessert Recipes 161

68.	Instant Pot Mini Keto Chocolate Mini Cakes	161
69.	Vanilla Bean Cheesecake	163
70.	Instant Pot Mini Molten Lava Cake	165

Conclusion 167
About the Author 168
Index 169

Introduction

The Instant Pot Mini

It's time to introduce you to the Instant Pot Mini! If you don't already know what it is then you are definitely in for a treat. The Instant Pot Mini is really a miracle cooker, it is an amazingly versatile piece of household appliance that has grown in popularity over the past years. This revolutionary multi-cooker comes equipped with 7 different functions. That's right you will literally be getting the abilities of 7 different home appliances with just on cooker.

This amazing 3-quart version of the Instant Pot allows you to cooks meals that would generally be made in a pressure cooker, slow cooker, steamer, rice cooker, warming pot, yogurt maker, and a sauté pan in a matter of minutes. It is the perfect device for busy couples, enthusiastic singles or smaller families.

Getting to Know Your Instant Pot Mini

- What you get in the box

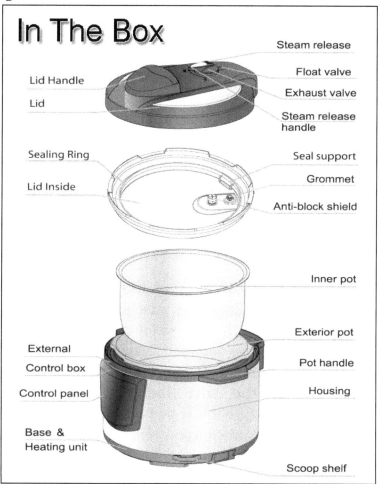

So, you have finally received your very own Instant Pot Mini, and you are about to open the box and use it for the very first time. We are just as excited as you are to dive into the box with you, and it definitely helps to know what to expect to receive in the box so that you are not left with a missing part. So, here's what you should expect to find when you open the box.

1. Cooking Equipment – You will get of course your Instant Pot Mini, this comes along with a steel lid, steel insert, steam rack, condensation collector, spatulas, and a measuring cup.
2. Documents
    - **User & Reference Guide** – Be sure to keep this guide handy and try to read it before actually using the Instant Pot Mini. This new appliance

carries so many features and has so many convenient settings that you may need to pull for it at some point.
- **Instant Pot Mini Collection of Recipes** – That's right your Instant Pot Mini comes equipped with a small recipe book to get you started, giving you an idea of
- **Information Sheet with Updates** – As the name suggests, this document tells you all the recent updates that have been made with your Instant Pot Mini. It is always recommended that you read this document before using the pot as functions of the cooker, and general usage may be upgraded, hence slightly different than you may be used to. A prime example of this is the recent updates in the slow cooking times that were adjusted after the manual had been created.

What To Do Before Your First Use

Now that you have unboxed your Instant Pot Mini here are 4 vital tips for you to follow before your first use.

1. **Remove, clean and reinstall the 'sealing' ring** – Your Instant Pot Mini comes equipped with a 'sealing' ring attached. It is recommended that you remove the ring and wash it with warm soapy water. Removing the 'sealing' is not hard at all. All you need to do is pull each section upwards from the 'sealing' ring, and it will pop right out. To reinstall simply press it back into place.
2. **Pull out and reinstall the Anti-Block Shield** – This may seem weird. However, it is recommended that you pull out the anti-block shield that comes installed into the Instant Pot Mini and reinstall it. This will ensure that it is properly installed. Once again, removing it is simple, all you need to do is push it on the side and lift it out. To reinstall simply set it back in to position and press it down.
3. **Set your condensation collector in place** – Your Instant Pot Mini will come a small cup that hooks onto the side of the pot. You want to avoid tossing this out as it can be very useful in the long run. It is meant to collect condensation drippings from your Instant Pot Mini while cooking and even cooling. This can come in extremely handy for protecting your beautiful wooden kitchen islands and counters, or at the very least save you a lot of cleaning. To install simply attach your condensation cup beneath the small hole slightly below the rim of your Instant Pot Mini.
4. Finally, **attach your power cord** and get cooking.

Understanding the Buttons of the Instant Pot Mini

1. **Slow Cook –**

This button allows you to transform your IP Mini into a slow cooker. There are three different modes low (cooking between 180–190°F), normal (cooking between 190–200°F), and high (cooking between 200–210°F).

2. **[+] & [-] buttons –**

These buttons are used to increase, set or decrease cook time.

3. **Pressure Level –**

This button allows you select your pressure settings. You can set the pressure levels to either High or Low and can be used with all the other cooking modes that allow for pressure control.

4. **Keep Warm –**

This button allows you to opt in or out of your IP Mini keeping your food warm at a temperature of 145–172°F for you after it has done cooking. It is important to note that this Keep Warm function is automatically on by default and so if you would not like to use this function be sure to switch it off when setting up to cook.

5. **Yogurt** –

This button is pretty self-explanatory, it allows you to make yogurt in your IP Mini. There are 2 settings for Yogurt 'More', used mainly when boiling your milk and 'Normal' generally used during the incubation process.

6. **Sauté** –

Yet another self-explanatory button, it allows you to sauté food in your IP Mini. Simply add in your ingredients once the IP Mini displays the word "Hot" on the screen and select either 'Normal', 'Less' or 'More'. 'Normal' mode is typically used for sautéing vegetables, 'More' may be more suited to browning meats, while the 'Less' setting can be used for simmering.

7. **Delay Start** –

As the name suggests this button allows you to delay the time in which your IP Mini begins cooking. To use it simply chose what cooking function you would like to use, adjust the timer to match the recipe then press the Delay Start button and choose a time interval in which you would like to wait before cooking using the [+] and [-] buttons.

8. **Cancel** –

This button will allow you stop the cooking program when needed.

9. **Pressure Cook** –

This button will become the button you use the most as it is a popular button among recipes. It replaced the 'Manual' button in some of the other models and allows you to use your IP Mini as a pressure cooker and cook using wither High or Low pressure.

Why You Need an Instant Pot Mini in Your Home?

- **To create healthy meals that are delicious**

One the main issues that is often experienced when cooking on the range top is the leaching. When it comes to food, this refers to when nutrients, and juices ooze out of the food that we cook due to the length of time that it takes to cook them on over the range. With an Instant Pot Mini, however, the issue of leaching is almost nonexistent as the pot allows you cook meats and fresh vegetables completely in only a few minutes, at a high temperature, in a covered pot. Due to this, there is no room for the juices or nutrients to escape so you will always be left with a delicious serving of juicy, and healthy food.

- **Perfect for any season**

Unlike other appliances that that you use at one specific event in the year then forget it to collect dust for the remaining season as there is simply nothing to cook with it, your instant cooker is so versatile it will never be forgotten. With an appliance this versatile you can enjoy simple meals at any time of the year from stews and soups during the winter, to delicious vegetable casseroles in the summer, and decadent desserts for the spring and fall. Your remaining appliances will soon become nonexistent.

- **Spend less time slaving in the kitchen**

Time is money! Most of us dread any meal that will leave us standing for hours to create, and as a result we end up opting for less nutritional meals or even takeout, but not anymore. One of the most inviting perks of creating meals in an Instant Pot Mini is the fact that it allows for leg room to relax and allow the appliance to handle the cooking. Gone are the days that you have to constantly stand over the pot stirring or checking constantly to ensure that whatever you are cooking doesn't bun. Most meals take very little to no effort to get it cooked as once the food in in the Instant Pot Mini and set to cook all you have to do is wait to enjoy the delicious meal that is being created.

Pressure Release Methods

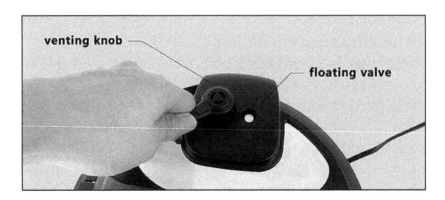

When you speak of pressure release you are referring to the method in which you use to release the pressure from the IP Mini. There are mainly 3 different types of pressure releases that are used with the Instant Pot Mini, namely:

1. **Quick Pressure Release** – which allows your Instant Pot Mini to quickly release the trapped pressure that is holding the cooker shut. To perform this method, you will need to carefully switch the pressure vent from 'sealing' position to 'venting'.
2. **Natural Pressure Release** – which simply put means that you allow the Instant Pot Mini to come to room temperature naturally without adjusting anything.
3. **Combination Pressure Release** – As the name suggests this is combination of both the quick release and natural release methods. Recipes that call for this method generally specify the times for each, the key thing to remember is that you typically allow the Instant Pot Mini to begin cooling down naturally then switching to the quick release method to finish the release process.

The Ketogenic Diet: The Basics

Ketogenic Dieting is far from novel in concept, with its practices having been presented in several forms and variations. Ketogenic diets share commonalities with the Atkin's Diet, and are similar to other popular diets, such as the South Beach and Paleo diets. In this blog, we'll detail the ketogenic diet and its underlying principle, while outlining its function, operations, and ways for you to get started.

Before we begin, we need to cover the bases by understanding the different categories of ketogenic diets that exist. The three types of ketogenic diets, which are very similar in nature, are the Standard Ketogenic Diet, the Targeted Ketogenic Diet and the Cyclical Ketogenic Diet. The basis upon which each category varies is carbohydrate consumption, regarding limits and timing. The general reference for ketogenic diets that we'll use is the website, TheKetogenicDiet.org, which, unless otherwise specified, points to the Standard Ketogenic diet. However, the information provided here is applicable to any of the three types of diets that you choose to follow.

Defining the Ketogenic Diet

Simply put, a ketogenic diet is one which leads the body to a state of ketosis, during which, to burn energy, the body is forced to utilize fats instead of carbohydrates. In order for this to occur, a ketogenic dieter must consume miniscule amounts of carbohydrates, sufficient amounts of proteins and a large amount of fats. By limiting the amount of carbohydrates, we consume, and hence, reaching a state of ketosis, we stimulate the liver's breakdown of fat cells into ketones and fatty acids (two possible sources of energy).

How Does the Ketogenic Diet Work?

Like most other diets, the ketogenic diet greatly relies on the limitation of calories, which, in turn, leads to more energy being burnt than that which is consumed. This principle is the fundamental basis upon which diets are proven successful, despite the fact that the "a calorie is a calorie" notion is still debatable.

One may ask why the ketogenic diet doesn't simply focus on calories, instead of cutting down carbs. If most diet books focus on reducing fats, recommended by nutritionists, then, what is the benefit of choosing a ketogenic diet?

To answer such an excellent question, ketogenic diets are based on hunger control, a factor that is not as effectively managed in many other diets.

Foods You Can Eat on a Ketogenic Diet

The mechanism of the ketogenic diet is based on the alternate use of fats as fuel when carbohydrate contents are minimized in the muscles. Using this process, known as ketosis, the body sheds weight very reliably and efficiently.

A state of ketosis requires a very low-carb diet, with probably no more than 20g per day within the first few weeks. Depending on your plan or the stage of your diet, your carb intake may be higher than this figure. Either way, your diet should be comprised of mostly fat, protein and green veggies as a source of nutritious carbs. Below is a list of foods we suggest for the ketogenic diet:

Ketogenic Diet Foods List:
- **Meat** of all kinds, preparations and cuts are fine once they're not cured with honey or sugar. These include veal, venison, pork, beef and lamb, but other meats such as sausages should be examined for their carbohydrate content.
- **Poultry, such as quail, duck, chicken and turkey,** is best cooked with its skin, since it adds to the fat content of the meat. Most methods of preparation, such as deep frying or baking are fine. However, battering and breading of poultry should be avoided.
- **Shellfish and fish** are best eaten fresh, and other fish like canned fish should be examined for preservatives. Products such as imitation crab, which contain added carbs, should be avoided, and breaded/battered fish and shellfish are not recommended.
- **Eggs**, as you'll realize, are a major go-to in this ketogenic diet.
- **Cheeses** of most kinds are a good addition to your daily carb intake. Just ensure that their inclusion does not cause you to exceed your carb limit.
- **Vegetables**, though safe, should also be weighed and bargained, as you would want to choose veggies of lowest carbs and most nutrition. Of the many that will comprise your carbohydrate quota, the green, leafy veggies are an absolute best. These include all types of lettuce and cabbage, kale, watercress, spinach, Brussel sprouts, radishes, celery, cucumber, bean sprouts, asparagus, cauliflower, and broccoli. However, there are more sugary vegetables, such as onions, tomatoes, peppers and potatoes (or other starchy veggies) that you should ensure that you eat only in minimal amounts.
- **Nuts** make good snacks and are to be eaten in moderate amounts.
- **Most oils**, such as butter and cream, are fine for cooking purposes.

- **Fresh herbs** and dry spices are good for adding flavor to your foods.
- **Salad dressings with oil bases and mayonnaise** are fine once you examine the carb content details, found on labels.
- **Artificial Sweeteners**, such as EZ-Sweets and Stevia, can be used, and they make great alternatives for sugar.

Foods to Avoid on a Ketogenic Diet

The ketogenic diet takes a little getting used to, since many concepts about dieting have been shifted around in your head. When it comes to diets, you may have thought that fats were a big No-No, which makes your adjustment to the keto lifestyle that much more confusing in concept. Perhaps you didn't know that some common foods were actually high-carb, and now, you've discovered that they should be avoided on this diet. You'll need to have guidance on the foods to stay away from, which is just what we'll discuss in this upcoming section.

What is a Carbohydrate?

Believe it or not, all carbohydrates are actually sugars, even though some carb-containing foods don't taste particularly sweet. Sugars are structurally simple carbohydrates, and make up structures like fructose, which is the sugar that gives fruits their sweet taste. Other foods, such as bread, rice, potato, pasta and other high carb foods, comprise of starches and other molecules that are more structurally complex. These foods, which are made up of several sugar chains, are acted upon by the enzyme amylase. Amylase in the stomach and saliva breaks down these carbohydrates into sugars, after which they are digested by the body. Proof of this mechanism would be found in bread, which comprises of starch that is broken down into sugars by salivary amylase. After chewing bread for an extended period of time, you can taste the slight sweetness as evidence of sugars.

What This Means

For you, this would mean greater scrutiny when it comes your carb count, as foods with sugars and starches contain carbohydrates as well. Foods that contain large amounts of sugars and starches should be avoided altogether. Therefore, foods like sweet vegetables (e.g. carrots and peppers), starchy vegetables (e.g. potatoes, swede, yams), starchy foods (e.g. pasta, bread, pastry and rice), and fruit should mostly be excluded from your ketogenic diet.

The Role of Fiber in The Ketogenic Diet

A carbohydrate that is welcomed by the ketogenic diet is fiber, as it can never be digested by the body nor its glucose absorbed by the bloodstream. As it passes through the body, it remains, to a large extent, unaltered, as it helps with the transport of other foods through the digestive system. For this reason, when carb content is calculated for a particular food, the value of its fiber is subtracted from the total figure.

Safety Considerations & Possible Side Effects of the Keto Diet

Although Keto dieting has been proven to have many health and weight-loss benefits, a sudden or abrupt transition can cause a few mild, short-term effects. These encompass:

Headaches and Dizziness

In the early stages of your ketogenic journey, you would have gotten rid of caffeine (in many cases, it can be later reincorporated) and sugar from your diet. Because of their commonly-known addictive properties, they tend to lead to you experiencing withdrawal symptoms. Symptoms of this caliber, however, last for just a couple of days, with mild effects and thereafter, no addictive signs or symptoms (physical). Therefore, after the initial effects of addiction, you will no longer experience the sensation of sugar or coffee to stay alert.

Leg Cramps

It is not unusual to have leg cramps when just starting the keto diet, especially with most instances occurring in the night time. Stemming from a lack of potassium, such cramps can be remedied by taking potassium-containing multivitamins. Whether or not you experience such side effects, the taking of multivitamins is encouraged to prevent deficiencies that may be caused by the diet's restrictions.

Constipation

A common mistake that ketogenic dieters make is to forget about fiber when it comes to their daily carb intake. A negative effect of insufficient amounts of fiber is constipation, which can be avoided by eating more green vegetables. In addition to these veggies, it is important to drink lots of water to prevent or help treat constipation. If you still find trouble treating your constipation, you can use a mild over-the-counter laxative to get rid of your problem.

Bad Breath

On a keto diet, your body burns fat for energy release, a process we have been referring to as ketosis. As part of this process, ketones are released in your breath and urine, and acetone, a particular ketone, possesses a specific smell. While the smell of acetone isn't necessarily malodorous (like in the case of bad or smelly breath that is caused by halitosis), you may notice a fruity candy or sugary smell. If you find it unpleasant, you can just use parsley, fresh mint, breath spray, sugar-free gum or mouthwash, any of which would do the trick.

My Cooking Tips

Now you've received your Instant Pot Mini, taken it out of the box, and you're prepared to cook your very first meal with it.

However, you're still feeling a bit intimidated by it.

It's perfectly fine!

It may be a bit overwhelming at first but as the proverb goes, "Practice makes a man perfect."

So here are a few suggestions to keep in mind as you begin to use your appliance.

1) Overfilling the Instant Pot
Do not fill your Instant Pot Mini with ingredients to the "Max Line" as this may end up clogging the Venting Knob. Use the two-third marker as a guide on the inside of the Instant Pot. If you have accidentally overfilled the pot, relax. Use the Natural Pressure Release and you'll be safe.

2) Cleaning the bottom of the Inner Pot
The Sauté does come in handy when you're handling recipes that call for ingredients to be browned. However, this may stain the bottom of your inner pot. So, make sure to scrape the bottom of your inner pot clean before switching functions.

3) Turn the Venting Knob to its Sealed Position
At the beginning, there may be a lot of steps for you to take when operating with the Instant Pot. It's common to see users forgetting to turn the Venting Knob to the Sealing Position when cooking. So, make it a habit and ensure that the Venting Knob is turned to its Sealed Position every time you start pressure cooking.

14-Day Meal Plan

Below I have put together a simple 14 Day meal plan that you can enjoy using a few of the recipes of this book in a combination that will help you transition into ketosis.

Day 1 - Monday

- **Breakfast:** Keto Friendly Quiche
- **Lunch:** Instant Pot Mini Buffalo Ranch Chicken with Dip
- **Dinner:** Asian Beef Pot Roast
- **Dessert:** Vanilla Bean Cheesecake

Day 2 - Tuesday

- **Breakfast:** Instant Pot Mini Scotch Eggs
- **Lunch:** Smokey Barbecue Beans
- **Dinner:** Instant Pot Mini Chicken Curry
- **Dessert:** Instant Pot Mini Keto Chocolate Mini Cakes

Day 3 - Wednesday

- **Breakfast:** Instant Pot Mini Rice Milk Porridge
- **Lunch:** Instant Pot Mini Carnitas Lettuce Wraps
- **Dinner:** Curried Chicken with Cauliflower
- **Dessert:** Instant Pot Mini Molten Lava Cake

Day 4 - Thursday

- **Breakfast:** Keto Friendly Quiche
- **Lunch:** Instant Pot Mini Buffalo Ranch Chicken with Dip
- **Dinner:** Asian Beef Pot Roast
- **Dessert:** Vanilla Bean Cheesecake

Day 5 - Friday

- **Breakfast:** Instant Pot Mini Scotch Eggs
- **Lunch:** Smokey Barbecue Beans
- **Dinner:** Instant Pot Mini Chicken Curry
- **Dessert:** Instant Pot Mini Keto Chocolate Mini Cakes

Day 6 - Saturday

- **Breakfast:** Instant Pot Mini Rice Milk Porridge
- **Lunch:** Instant Pot Mini Carnitas Lettuce Wraps
- **Dinner:** Curried Chicken with Cauliflower
- **Dessert:** Instant Pot Mini Molten Lava Cake

Day 7 - Sunday

- **Breakfast:** Keto Friendly Quiche
- **Lunch:** Instant Pot Mini Buffalo Ranch Chicken with Dip
- **Dinner:** Asian Beef Pot Roast
- **Dessert:** Vanilla Bean Cheesecake

Day 8 - Monday

- **Breakfast:** Instant Pot Mini Scotch Eggs
- **Lunch:** Smokey Barbecue Beans
- **Dinner:** Instant Pot Mini Chicken Curry
- **Dessert:** Instant Pot Mini Keto Chocolate Mini Cakes

Day 9 - Tuesday

- **Breakfast:** Instant Pot Mini Rice Milk Porridge
- **Lunch:** Instant Pot Mini Carnitas Lettuce Wraps
- **Dinner:** Curried Chicken with Cauliflower
- **Dessert:** Instant Pot Mini Molten Lava Cake

Day 10 - Wednesday.

- **Breakfast:** Keto Friendly Quiche
- **Lunch:** Instant Pot Mini Buffalo Ranch Chicken with Dip
- **Dinner:** Asian Beef Pot Roast
- **Dessert:** Vanilla Bean Cheesecake

Day 11 - Thursday

- **Breakfast:** Instant Pot Mini Scotch Eggs
- **Lunch:** Smokey Barbecue Beans
- **Dinner:** Instant Pot Mini Chicken Curry
- **Dessert:** Instant Pot Mini Keto Chocolate Mini Cakes

Day 12 - Friday

- **Breakfast:** Instant Pot Mini Rice Milk Porridge
- **Lunch:** Instant Pot Mini Carnitas Lettuce Wraps
- **Dinner:** Curried Chicken with Cauliflower
- **Dessert:** Instant Pot Mini Molten Lava Cake

Day 13 - Saturday

- **Breakfast** Keto Friendly Quiche
- **Lunch:** Instant Pot Mini Buffalo Ranch Chicken with Dip
- **Dinner:** Asian Beef Pot Roast
- **Dessert:** Vanilla Bean Cheesecake

Day 14 - Sunday

- **Breakfast:** Instant Pot Mini Scotch Eggs
- **Lunch:** Smokey Barbecue Beans
- **Dinner:** Instant Pot Mini Chicken Curry
- **Dessert:** Instant Pot Mini Keto Chocolate Mini Cakes

Instant Pot Mini Breakfast Recipes

1. Keto Friendly Quiche

Serves: 2
Prep Time: 10 minutes
Cook Time: 30 minutes
Release Mode: Natural
Release Time: 20 Minutes

Ingredients
- 1 cup water
- 3 whole eggs
- ¼ cup milk
- Pinch of salt and pepper
- 1 tablespoon of chives, chopped
- ½ a cup of cheddar cheese, shredded
- Cooking spray as needed

Directions
1. Add your milk, chives, pepper, salt and egg to a bowl then whisk until completely combined.
2. Wrap a cake pan with tin foil and grease with cooking spray then add cheese.
3. Top with your egg mixture and spread.
4. Pour water directly into your Instant Pot then fit in the steamer basket.

5. Add cake pan and close lid.
6. Ensure the pressure vent is set to 'Sealing' position then press the 'Pressure Cook' button and allow to cook on HIGH pressure for 30 minutes.
7. Do a natural release for about 20 minutes before attempting to open.
8. Serve and enjoy!

Nutrition (Per Serving)
Calories: 214
Fat: 4g
Carbohydrates: 7g
Protein: 8g

2. Instant Pot Mini Scotch Eggs

Serves: 4
Prep Time: 20 Minutes
Cook Time: 30 Minutes
Release Mode: Quick
Release Time: 10 Minutes

Ingredients
- 4 large eggs
- 1 lb., ground Sausage
- 1 tbsp. Avocado oil
- 2 cups water

Directions
1. Add a cup of water to the steel insert of your Instant Pot Mini, then gently add your eggs.
2. Press the 'Pressure Cook' button and set the timer for 6 minutes.
3. When the timer goes off, press the cancel button and perform a quick pressure release by opening the valve to allow the trapped steam to release more quickly.
4. Once cool, carefully open. Remove the steel insert and transfer your eggs to a bowl of cold water so that it cools completely.
5. Once cool, deshell your eggs and evenly wrap your sausage meat around your four boiled eggs.
6. Dry your steel insert and replace it in the cooker base.

7. Set your Instant Pot Mini to "sauté" mode by pressing the 'Sauté' button and add your oil once the pot gets hot.
8. Proceed to brown your Scotch eggs evenly on all sides then remove and set aside.
9. Next, add a cup water in your insert and fit a rack into the steel basket.
10. Add your browned eggs on the rack and set your timer to 6 minutes and allow to cook.
11. Once done, again perform a quick pressure release, and carefully open your Instant Pot Mini. Enjoy!

Nutrition (Per Serving)
Calories: 270
Fat: 16.6g
Carbs: 16.9g
Protein: 11.1g

3. Instant Pot Mini Hard-Boiled Eggs

Serves: 2
Prep Time: 10 Minutes
Cook Time: 5 Minutes
Release Mode: Natural
Release Time: 10 Minutes

Ingredients
- 4 large eggs
- 1 cup water

Directions
1. Add a cup of water to the steel insert of your Instant cooker, then gently add your eggs.
2. Press the 'Pressure Cook' button and set the timer for 5 minutes.
3. When the timer goes off, press the cancel button and allow to cool down naturally for about 10 minutes before attempting to open.
4. Once cool, carefully open. Remove the steel insert and transfer your eggs to a bowl of cold water until they are cool enough to touch.
5. Once cool, deshell your eggs, serve and enjoy.

Nutrition (Per Serving)
Calories: 60
Fat: 4g
Carbs: 1.1g
Protein: 6g

4. Instant Pot Mini Rice Milk Porridge

Serves: 4
Prep Time: 5 Minutes
Cook Time: 25 Minutes
Release Mode: Natural
Release Time: 10 Minutes

Ingredients
- ¼ cup Xanthan gum
- 3 cups Rice milk
- 1, sliced Banana
- ¼ cup Raisins
- 1 tsp., ground Cinnamon
- 1 tsp., ground Nutmeg
- ½ tsp. Vanilla

Directions
1. Fit your steel basket into your Instant Pot Mini.
2. In a medium bowl, combine your xanthan gum and 2 cups of your rice milk and whisk until no lumps remain.
3. Add all your remaining ingredients to the Instant Pot Mini, press the 'Sauté' button, set on high then allow to come to a boil.
4. Once boiling, carefully stir in your xanthan gum and rice milk mixture.

5. Stir until no lumps remain then switch your Instant Pot Mini to the porridge by pressing the 'Porridge' button then allow to cook on low with your timer set to 6 minutes.
6. When done, allow your cooker to cool down naturally for about 20 minutes before attempting to open.
7. Carefully open the lid and serve. Enjoy!

Nutrition (Per Serving)
Calories: 88
Fat: 2 g
Carbs: 16g
Protein: 2 g

5. Chocolate Zucchini Muffin Bites

Serves: 3
Prep Time: 15 Minutes
Cook Time: 8 Minutes
Release Mode: Natural
Release Time: 20 Minutes

Ingredients
- 1 egg
- ½ cup, evaporated Cane juice
- ¼ cup Coconut oil
- 1 tsp. Vanilla extract
- ½ tbsp. melted Butter
- 1 ½ tbsp. Cocoa Powder
- ½ cup Almond flour
- ½ tbsp. Xanthan Gum
- ¼ tsp. Baking soda
- 1/8 tsp. Salt
- ¼ tsp. Cinnamon
- ½ cup, grated Zucchini
- ½ cup water

Directions
1. In a medium bowl add your sweetener, eggs, vanilla, and coconut oil, then whisk to combine.
2. Combine your cocoa powder and butter in a separate bowl and whisk until a dark paste like substance is formed.
3. Next, add your cocoa mixture to your egg mixture and whisk to combine.
4. Once combined, add all your dry ingredients and fold to combine.
5. Fit your Instant Pot Mini with your steel insert, and a trivet then add your water and set the cooker on the sauté setting to allow it to preheat.
6. Fill up silicone muffin cups ⅔ way full with your muffin batter and set your muffin cups to set on top of the trivet you fitted into the cooker.
7. Prep a cover by cutting a piece of parchment paper and aluminum foil to create a circle then use to cover your muffin cups.
8. Set your Instant Pot Mini to pressure by pressing the 'Pressure Cook' button and cook on high for 8 minutes.
9. Once your timer has finished, press the 'Cancel' button and allow your IP Mini to cook down naturally for about 15 to 20 minutes before attempting to open.
10. Test your muffins for doneness as you would a cake. Finally, serve and enjoy.

Nutrition (Per Serving)
Calories: 107
Fat: 3g
Carbs: 16g
Protein: 4g

Instant Pot Mini Lunch Recipes

6. Keto Instant Pot Mini Snow Peas & Bell Pepper

Serves: 4
Prep Time: 5 Minutes
Cook Time: 15 Minutes
Release Mode: Natural
Release Time: 20 Minutes

Ingredients
- 1 tbsp. olive oil
- 4 shiitake mushrooms, cut into halves
- 1 red bell pepper, seeded and sliced
- 1 garlic, minced
- 3 tbsp. water
- 8oz. snow peas
- Salt and pepper, to taste

Directions:
1. Set your Instant Pot Mini to preheat on "sauté" mode by pressing the 'Sauté' button.
2. Once hot, add the oil. Add garlic and cook until fragrant.
3. Next, add the mushrooms and cook for 3 minutes.
4. Add the snow peas and gradually add the water.
5. Close the lid, and make sure that your pressure valve is set to "sealing."
6. Set the Instant Pot Mini to cook on "pressure" mode by pressing the 'Pressure Cook' button with low pressure for about 3 minutes.
7. When the timer ends, allow the Instant Pot Mini to cool down naturally for at least 20 minutes before trying to open.
8. Open lid and add the sliced bell peppers. Stir to combine.
9. Reheat your Instant Pot Mini on "sauté" mode by pressing the 'Sauté' button and allow your bell peppers to cook until they become fork tender (about 5 minutes).
10. Season to taste and serve.

Nutrition (Per Serving)
Calories: 41.2
Fat: 0.2 g
Carbs: 7.4 g
Protein: 9.5g

7. Instant Pot Mini Spaghetti Squash

Serves: 2
Prep Time: 5 Minutes
Cook Time: 20 Minutes
Release Mode: Quick
Release Time: 10 Minutes

Ingredients
- 1 medium spaghetti squash
- 1 cup water
- Sprinkle of salt and pepper

Directions
1. Cut the spaghetti squash crosswise, in half with a paring knife. You'll get longer strands of spaghetti squash if you cut it in half crosswise.
2. Scoop out the seeds in the center of the squash with a large spoon and throw away the gunk.
3. Into your Instant Pot Mini place, the steamer insert and pour a cup of water in the pot.
4. Place the squash on the steamer insert anyway desired. Cover pressure cooker and cook for 7 minutes under high pressure.
5. Press the 'Pressure Cook' button, hold the plus or minus button until display changes to 7.

6. Do a quick pressure release for about 10 minutes. Pour out excess water from cooker by removing the lid and tilt the halves of the squash.
7. Check on the readiness by sticking the squash with a fork (Squash should be toothsome, not squishy).
8. If you desire your squash to be more tender cook on high pressure for a further 3 minutes.
9. Remove squash from pot and shred with a fork. Your Spaghetti squash is now ready. Go for it!

Nutrition (Per Serving)
Calories: 31
Fat: 0.6 g
Carbs: 7 g
Protein: 0.6 g

8. Instant Pot Mini Carnitas Lettuce Wraps

Serves: 4
Total Time: 45 Minutes
Prep Time: 30 Minutes
Cook Time: 15 Minutes
Release Mode: Quick
Release Time: 10 Minutes

Ingredients

- ½ tsp. Onion salt
- ½ tbsp., unsweetened Cocoa powder
- 1 tsp. salt
- ½ tsp. Cayenne pepper
- 1 tsp., dried Oregano
- ½ tsp. Garlic powder
- ½ tsp., ground Cumin
- ½ tsp. White pepper
- 1.5 lbs. Pork
- 1 tbsp. Olive oil
- 1.5 cups water
- ¼ tsp., ground Coriander
- ½ head, washed and dried Butter lettuce
- 1 small, sliced Jalapeño
- 1/8 cup, julienned Radishes

- ½ Avocado
- 1 small, diced Roma tomato
- 1, cut into wedges Lime

Directions
1. Add your cayenne pepper, cocoa powder, salt, white pepper, oregano, onion salt, cumin, coriander, and garlic powder, in a small bowl.
2. Use the mixture to season your pork. Let rest in the refrigerator covered overnight.
3. Set your Instant Pot Mini to "sauté" mode by pressing the 'Sauté' button.
4. Add your oil, then roast and brown on all sides until fully browned (this should take 10 minutes).
5. Add enough water to cover meat. Close the lid and set your pressure valve to "sealing." Set to pressure mode by pressing the 'Pressure Cook' button and allow to cook for 45 minutes.
6. When the timer ends, do a quick release by carefully switching the pressure valve from 'sealed' to 'venting.' This will allow your Instant Pot Mini to release the trapped pressure that is holding the cooker shut.
Tip: Be extremely careful as you do this as the Instant Pot Mini will be hot, and the steam released can also burn your hands. Consider using an oven mitten or pot holder.
7. Open, and take your pork from the Instant Pot Mini to a platter.
8. Shred the meat with two forks. Drain the liquid from the Instant Pot Mini into a bowl.
9. Discard a half of the liquid and add back your meat to the pot.
10. Add your reserved liquid and set to "sauté" mode by pressing the 'Sauté' button.
11. Stir-fry until crispy. Serve, and enjoy!

Nutrition (Per Serving)
Calories: 176
Fat: 5 g
Carbs:14 g
Protein: 18.5 g

9. Instant Pot Mini Ham

Serves: 4
Prep Time: 5 Minutes
Cook Time: 15 Minutes
Release Mode: Natural
Release Time: 20 Minutes

Ingredients
- ¼ cup water
- 2lb., bone-in Ham

GLAZE:
- 1/8 cup Stevia

OPTIONAL INGREDIENTS FOR GLAZE:
- 1 tsp. Dijon mustard
- 1 tsp. Worcestershire sauce
- ¼ tsp. Cinnamon
- 1/8 tsp., ground Ginger
- ¼ tsp., freshly grated Nutmeg
- 1/8 tsp., ground Cloves

Directions
1. Prepare your Instant Pot Mini by adding about ¼ cup water into your Instant Pot Mini's basin. Add your ham in the basin cut side down.

Tip: Consider cutting the ham in half if it is too big to hold in your Instant Pot Mini and cooking two batches.

2. Add all your glaze ingredients together in a medium bowl, and whisk to combine.
3. Add over ham, close your Instant Pot Mini lid, and set your pressure value to "sealing."
4. Press the 'Pressure Cook' button and allow to cook on high for 10 minutes.
5. When the time runs out, allow your Instant Pot Mini to cool down naturally (without adjusting the pressure valve) for at least 20 minutes before trying to open.
6. Transfer the liquid remaining in the pot to a bowl then set aside. Remove your ham from the pot and set aside.
7. Return your Instant Pot Mini to "sauté" mode by pressing the 'Sauté' button on the highest setting.
8. Pour the reserved pot water back into the pot and allow to reduce into a semi thick sauce.
9. Slice your ham and serve with sweet sauce.

Nutritional (Per Serving)
Calories: 337
Fat: 17 g
Carbs: 11 g
Protein: 29 g

10. Instant Pot Mini Chili Lime Steak Bowl

Serves: 4
Prep Time: 5 Minutes
Cook Time: 15 Minutes
Release Mode: Quick
Release Time: 10 Minutes

Ingredients
- 1.2-2 pounds of fajita steak strips
- 1 tablespoon of water
- 1 teaspoon minced garlic
- 1 tablespoon of Extra Virgin Olive Oil
- 2 teaspoons of lime juice
- ½ teaspoon chili powder
- ½ teaspoon sea salt
- ½ teaspoon cracked pepper
- 1 teaspoon of Cholula
- 2-3 Avocado diced

Directions
1. Turn your IP Mini on sauté and add olive oil. Once hot, add garlic and cook until a golden color. Then add all remaining ingredients and mix well with wooden spoon.
2. Close your lid and set your Instant Pot Mini on pressure mode by pressing the 'Pressure Cook' with HIGH Pressure and allow to cook for about 10 minutes.

3. When the timer ends, do a quick release by carefully switching the pressure valve from 'sealed' to 'venting.' This will allow your Instant Pot Mini to release the trapped pressure that is holding the cooker shut.
   Tip: Be extremely careful as you do this as the Instant Pot Mini will be hot, and the steam released can also burn your hands. Consider using an oven mitten or pot holder.
4. Once pressure is released, removed lid. Turn pan back onto sauté mode and stir the meat to break it up into little chunks.
5. Keep on sauté mode by pressing the 'Sauté' button until liquid has been reduced by half. Allow to cool and serve in a bowl, and then surround it with your diced avocado. Yum!

Nutritional (Per Serving)
Calories: 292
Fat: 10.4 g
Carbs: 46 g
Protein: 10 g

11. Low-Carb Green Chile Pork Taco Bowl

Serves: 2-3
Prep Time: 15 Minutes
Cook Time: 45 Minutes
Release Mode: Natural
Release Time: 20 Minutes

Ingredients
- 1 lb. Pork sirloin roast
- 1 tsp. Ground cumin
- 1 tsp. Garlic powder
- ½ tsp. Salt
- ½ tsp. Black pepper
- ½ tsp. Olive oil
- ½ tin Green chili tomatillo salsa

For Serving:
- Best Easy Cauliflower Rice
- ½ large, finely chopped Poblano Chile Pepper
- ½ tsp. Lime juice
- Mexican blend cheese (grated)

- sour cream
- taco toppings (as desired)

Directions:
1. Trim the pork roast to remove excess fat and slice in thick pieces. Cut pork against the grain in order to get proper pieces when pork is shredded later.
2. Season meat with powdered seasoning and rub in properly. Brown meat over medium-high flame until both sides are golden brown.
3. Put pork at the bottom of the Instant Pot Mini. Cover pork in the tomatillo salsa. Seal the lid and set on 'Pressure Cook' for 45 minutes using HIGH pressure.
4. Use natural release for not less than 20 minutes when the time expires then using quick release, release the rest of the pressure.
5. Transfer pork to a cutting board and shred apart. Return meat to Instant Pot Mini and select keep warm.
6. During the cooking of the meat follow directions to make Best Easy Cauliflower Rice.
7. Sauté Poblano chili pepper for a brief period in the olive oil just after garlic pieces are removed then add in your cauliflower rice.
8. When serving, serve cauliflower rice mixture at the bottom of a serving bowl topped with a large amount of the spicy, delicious pork mixture.
9. If desired, drizzle lime juice; add sour cream, and grated Mexican Blend Cheese topped with any other desired taco toppings.

Nutritional (Per Serving)
Calories: 128
Fat: 1 g
Carbs: 25 g
Protein: 7 g

12. Instant Pot Mini Keema

Serves: 3
Prep Time: 15 Minutes
Cook Time: 50 Minutes
Release Mode: Natural
Release Time: 20 Minutes

Ingredients
- 1 tbsp. ghee
- ½ finely chopped onion
- 2 cloves garlic
- 1-inch ginger
- 1 serrano pepper
- ½ tbsp. coriander powder
- ½ tsp. paprika
- ½ tsp. salt
- ¼ tsp. turmeric
- ¼ tsp. black pepper
- ¼ tsp. garam masala
- ¼ tsp. cumin powder
- 1/8 tsp. Cayenne pepper
- 1/8 tsp. ground cardamom

- ½ lb. ground beef
- 7 oz. diced tomatoes
- 1 cup Peas
- Cilantro (for taste)

Directions
1. Add onions and ghee to the Instant Pot Mini. On the Instant Pot Mini, press the 'Sauté' button and set for 7 -10 mins, or until the onions begin to change slightly to brown.
2. Next, add the spices, ginger, garlic and serrano pepper and Sauté for minimum of 30 sec. Next, add the beef.
3. Cook until the outside of the beef is mostly brown. Stir in the can peas and the diced tomatoes.
4. On the Instant Pot Mini, cover and secure the lid and push the 'Cancel' button then the 'Bean/Chili' button and start pressuring.
5. Time will naturally be set for 30 minutes. Ensure the pressure valve is set sealing.
6. The Instant Pot Mini will automatically go the "keep warm" mode once meat is finished.
7. Please allow pressure to naturally release for about 20 minutes.
8. If a lot of extra fluid is released from the meat, select the 'Sauté' button to reduce the extra liquid it may take 15- 20 mins based on the amount of fluid. Enjoy!

Nutritional (Per Serving)
Calories: 257
Fat: 20.4 g
Carbs: 3.2 g
Protein: 15 g

13. Instant Pot Mini Pork Carnitas

Serves: 4
Prep Time: 20 Minutes
Cook Time: 50 Minutes
Release Mode: Natural
Release Time: 20 Minutes

Ingredients
- 3 lbs. trimmed boneless pork shoulder
- 2 tsp. kosher salt
- black pepper (pinch)
- garlic (6 cloves, cut in lengthwise slices)
- 1 tsp. cumin
- ½ tsp. sazon (1/2 tsp.)
- ¼ tsp. dry oregano (1/4 tsp.)
- ¾ cup, low sodium chicken broth
- 3 chipotle peppers in adobo sauce (to taste)
- 2 bay leaves
- ¼ tsp. dry adobo seasoning
- ½ tsp. garlic powder

Directions

1. Rub in salt and pepper on pork shoulder. In a large Dutch pot or skillet, brown all sides of pork on high heat. Remove from pot and set aside to cool.
2. Puncture pork with a sharp knife, puncture pork with 1-inch deep holes and insert garlic slices into them.
3. Season pork all over with dried oregano, sazon, oregano, cumin, adobo seasoning and garlic powder.
4. In an Instant Pot Mini, pour chicken broth, stir in chipotle peppers; add bay leaves.
5. Place seasoned pork in the Pot, cover lid, press the 'Pressure Cook' button and cook on HIGH pressure for fifty minutes on the meat button.
6. Please allow pressure to naturally release for about 20 minutes.
7. After the pressure is released, shred pork (this can be done by using two forks) and mix well with the juices that built up in the pot from the pork.
8. Remove bay leaves, add dried adobo and adjust cumin to taste, mix well.
9. Serve with fresh tortillas and salsa. Perfect for taco salads, burrito bowls and much more.

Nutritional (Per Serving)

Calories: 160
Fat: 7 g
Carbs: 1 g
Protein: 20 g

14. Keto Pressure Cooker Garlic Butter Chicken

Serves: 4
Prep Time: 5 Minutes
Cook Time: 40 Minutes
Release Mode: Natural
Release Time: 20 Minutes

Ingredients
- 4 pcs, whole or diced chicken breasts
- ¼ cup ghee
- 1 tsp. turmeric powder
- 1 tsp. salt (add more to taste)
- garlic (10 cloves, peeled and diced)

Directions
1. Clean and wash chicken breasts then place chicken in your Instant Pot Mini.
2. Press the 'Pressure Cook' button then in pressure mode, combine turmeric, ghee, diced garlic and salt, set on HIGH pressure, and cook for about 30 minutes.
3. When the timer ends, allow the Instant Pot Mini to cool down naturally for about 20 minutes. Carefully remove the lid.
4. Let the chicken remain in the pot and shred. Serve, (additional ghee can be added if needed).

Nutritional (Per Serving)
Calories: 404
Fat: 21 g
Carbs: 3 g
Protein: 47 g

Instant Pot Mini Snack Recipes

15.   Instant Pot Mini Cauliflower Mash

Serves: 4
Prep Time: 1 Minutes
Cook Time: 5 Minutes
Release Mode: Quick
Release Time: 10 Minutes

Ingredients
- 1 large head Cauliflower
- 1 cup water
- 1 tbsp., butter (optional)
- 1/8 tsp. salt
- 1/8 tsp. pepper
- ¼ tsp. Garlic powder
- Chives (handful, optional)
- 1 Steamer basket
- 1 Instant Pot Mini

Directions

1. Core the cauliflower and cut it into big chunks. Pour water into the Instant Pot Mini, place steamer basket in and add cauliflower.
2. Close your lid and set your IP Mini to pressure mode by pressing the 'Pressure Cook' button, set on HIGH pressure, and allow to cook for about 1 hour.
3. When the timer ends, do a quick release by carefully switching the pressure valve from 'sealed' to 'venting.' This will allow your Instant Pot Mini to release the trapped pressure that is holding the cooker shut.
Tip: Be extremely careful as you do this as the Instant Pot Mini will be hot, and the steam released can also burn your hands. Consider using an oven mitten or pot holder.
4. Use caution to remove the inner pot which drains water.
5. Put back cauliflower in a clean, empty inner pot. Now add salt, chives, butter, pepper, and garlic powder.
6. Puree using an immersion blender to consistency desired.
7. Stir and serve. Enjoy!

Nutrition (Per Serving)

Calories: 61
Fat: 1 g
Carbs: 10 g
Protein: 5 g

16. Instant Pot Mini Buffalo Ranch Chicken with Dip

Serves: 3 - 4
Prep Time: 2 Minutes
Cook Time 15 Hours
Release Mode: Quick
Release Time: 10 Minutes

Ingredients
- ½ lb. Chicken breast
- ½ packet of Ranch dip
- ½ tsp. Hot sauce
- 4 oz. butter
- 8 oz. Cheddar cheese
- 4 oz. Cream cheese

Directions
1. Add all your ingredients, except cheddar cheese, in your Instant Pot Mini and set to cook on the pressure setting by pressing the 'Pressure Cook' button for 15 minutes with high pressure.
2. When the timer ends, do a quick release by carefully switching the pressure valve from 'sealed' to 'venting.' This will allow your Instant Pot Mini to release the trapped pressure that is holding the cooker shut.

Tip: Be extremely careful as you do this as the Instant Pot Mini will be hot, and the steam released can also burn your hands. Consider using an oven mitten or pot holder.

3. Shred chicken with a fork or use your mixer to break it up.
4. Add your cheddar cheese and chicken to the pot and stir to melt cheese.
5. Serve, and enjoy.

Nutrition (Per Serving)
Calories: 108
Fat: 7.7 g
Carbs: 0.8 g
Protein: 7.2 g

17. Smokey Barbecue Beans

Serves: 4
Prep Time: 5 Minutes
Cook Time: 17 Minutes
Release Mode: Quick
Release Time: 10 Minutes

Ingredients
- 2 tbsp. Ghee
- 2 onions (diced)
- 2 tsp., minced Garlic
- 2 tsp., minced Ginger

Spices
- 2 tsp. salt
- 1 tsp. Coriander
- 1 tsp., ground Cumin
- 1 tsp. Garam masala
- ½ tsp. Black pepper
- ½ tsp. Cayenne
- ½ tsp. Turmeric
- 1 lb. rinsed Spinach
- 1 lb. rinsed Mustard leaves
- 1 tsp. Ghee

Directions
1. Set your Instant Pot Mini to preheat on "sauté" mode by pressing the 'Sauté' button.
2. Add in your ghee and allow to melt. As soon as it melts add ginger, onion, spices, and garlic, and continue to cook for about 3 minutes.
3. Add in your remaining ingredients and cook until it begins to wilt.
4. Close your lid and set your pressure valve to "sealing."
5. Set on "pressure" mode by pressing the 'Pressure Cook button', set on HIGH pressure, and allow to cook for about 15 minutes.
6. When the timer ends, do a quick release by carefully switching the pressure valve from 'sealed' to 'venting.' This will allow your Instant Pot Mini to release the trapped pressure that is holding the cooker shut.
   Tip: Be extremely careful as you do this as the Instant Pot Mini will be hot, and the steam released can also burn your hands. Consider using an oven mitten or pot holder.
7. Open, and process with an immersion blender. Serve with more ghee. Enjoy.

Nutrition (Per Serving)
Calories: 60
Fat: 3 g
Carbs:6 g
Protein: 2 g

18. Brussels Sprouts

Serves: 4
Prep Time: 10 Minutes
Cook Time: 16 Minutes
Release Mode: Quick
Release Time: 10 Minutes

Ingredients
- 4 cups Brussel sprouts
- 4 slices of bacon
- 4 oz. water
- 1 tbsp. honey
- sea salt (Habanero)

Directions
1. Slice the bacon slices into 1-inch squares. Cut the butts off the Brussel sprout and slice each in half. If there are fallen leaves, that's good because that will be crispier.
2. Trim up Brussel sprouts. Press the 'Sauté' button on your Instant Pot Mini, place the bacon slices in. Cook bacon for 7 mins., stirring at intervals to prevent it from burning.
3. After the time is up, place Brussels in the pot and sauté for 5 mins. more. Cook Brussels at the outer edges of the pot.

4. When cooking the bacon, the fat from it goes on the outside edge because it is lower. You get a crispier Brussel when it is done at that section. Stir Brussels occasionally to prevent burning.
5. Pour water in pot when the 5 minutes have expired. Shut off the sauté function, cover and ensure the lid is locked in place then set pressure valve to sealing.
6. Cook at HIGH pressure by pressing the 'Pressure Cook' button and setting to 2 1/2 minutes.
   NB: There will be a short delay to hit 'high pressure,' before it cooks for 2 1/2 minutes.
7. As soon as the timer goes off, carefully perform a quick release by switching the pressure valve to venting. This allows your Instant Pot Mini to release pressure quickly.
   Tip: Be extremely careful as you do this as the Instant Pot Mini will be hot, and the steam released can also burn your hands. Consider using an oven mitten or pot holder.
8. Transfer the vegetables to another container, sprinkle with the Habanero salt (has a touch of spice, just a pinch will do) and honey. Serve!

Nutritional (Per Serving)
Calories: 94
Fat: 4 g
Carbs: 11 g
Protein: 5 g

19. Prosciutto-wrapped Asparagus Canes

Serves: 2
Prep Time: 5 Minutes
Cook Time: 7 Minutes
Release Mode: Natural
Release Time: 20 Minutes

Ingredients
- Asparagus (1lb, thick)
- Prosciutto (8oz, thinly sliced)

Directions:
1. Prepare your Instant Pot Mini by pouring water in it (about 2 cups) and fit your steamer basket into the Instant Pot Mini. Set aside.
2. Begin by wrapping your asparagus in prosciutto and laying them in a singer layer at the bottom of your steamer basket.
   Tip: If you had any leftover asparagus, add them to the bottom of the steamer basket before adding in your wrapped ones as this will help prevent the prosciutto from sticking.
3. Close the lid, and make sure that your pressure valve is set to "sealing."
4. Set the Instant Pot Mini to cook on "pressure" mode by pressing the "Pressure Cook' button with HIGH pressure for about 3 minutes.

5. When the timer ends, allow the Instant Pot Mini to cool down naturally for at least 20 minutes before trying to open. Serve warm.

Nutritional (Per Serving)
Calories: 56
Fat: 4 g
Carbs: 3 g
Protein: 4 g

20. Steamed Artichokes

Serves: 1 - 2
Prep Time: 5 Minutes
Cook Time: 20 Minutes
Release Mode: Combination
Release Time: 10 Mins. Natural & 5 Mins. Quick

Ingredients
- artichokes (whole, enough to fit upright in one layer, trimmed)
- lemon (1 wedge)
- 1 cup water

Directions
1. Use lemon wedge to rub the top of each artichoke. This will prevent browning.
2. Place steamer basket or steam rack into the cooking insert of the Instant Pot Mini.
3. Put the artichokes on top and add a cup of water. Close the lid and set the valve in sealed position.
4. Use the 'Pressure Cook' button to set on pressure mode, let HIGH Pressure setting remain and adjust time according to the size of the artichokes.
NB: Allow 5 mins. for small artichokes, 10 mins. for medium size and 15 minutes for the large sizes.

5. After artichokes have completed cooking, use the combination release method and allow 10 mins. to lapse before opening the pressure valve to release any pressure remaining.
6. Remove artichokes (preferably with thongs) from cooker, serve warm with the dipping sauce desired. Enjoy!

Nutritional (Per Serving)
Calories: 64
Fat: 0.4 g
Carbs: 14.2 g
Protein: 4 g

21. Instant Pot Mini Cottage Cheese

Yields: 2 cups
Prep Time: 15 Minutes
Cook Time: 1 Hour 6 Minutes
Release Mode: Natural
Release Time: 20 minutes

Ingredients
- Milk (1 gallon, whole)
- Vinegar (3/4 cup, white)

Directions
1. Add a half of your milk to your Instant Pot Mini and set the remainder aside.
2. Cover your Instant Pot Mini and switch your pressure valve to sealing. Press the button that says 'Yogurt' twice so that the IP Mini displays BOILING.
3. Allow your milk to go through the whole boiling process. When your boiling process ends, press the 'Yogurt' button once more to adjust the Instant Pot Mini yogurt mode.
4. Allow to run in this mode for about an hour. Allow pressure to naturally release for about 20 minutes.
5. Open your Instant Pot Mini, and slowly add your vinegar and stir. Continue to stir as your milk curdles.

6. Continue to mix until your whey becomes a greenish color and begins to separate from the milk.
7. After you get to this point, use a mesh strainer to strain the whey from the cottage cheese.
8. Discard the whey and stir in your remaining milk to the cottage cheese until creamy.
9. Pour the mixture into an airtight container. Allow your cottage cheese to rest in the refrigerator until the best by date on the milk container. Enjoy!

Nutritional (Per Serving)
Calories: 98
Fat: 4.3 g
Carbs: 3.4 g
Protein: 11 g

Nutritional (Per Serving)
Calories: 160
Fat: 7 g
Carbs: 1 g
Protein: 20 g

Instant Pot Mini Dinner Recipes

22. Curried Chicken with Cauliflower

Serves: 8
Prep Time: 20 Minutes
Cook Time: 30 Minutes
Release Mode: Natural
Release Time: 20 Minutes

Ingredients
For the marinade:
- 4 lbs. Chicken leg quarters (4 lbs.)
- 1 tsp. Garlic powder (1 tsp.)
- 1 tsp. Onion powder (1 tsp.)
- 1 tbsp. Spicy yellow curry powder (1 tbsp.)
- 2 tbsp. Olive oil (2 tbsp.)
- 1 tsp. Kosher salt (1 tsp)

For the curry:
- 2 cups of coconut milk
- 1 tbsp. spicy yellow curry powder
- 1 cup water
- 3 cups cauliflower (cut into 1 ½" chunks)

- ¼ cup of chopped dates
- ¼ cup of chopped cilantro (for garnish)
- ¼ cup of fresh jalapeños (for garnish)

Directions
1. Wash and season chicken with marinade ingredients (except oil). Leave to marinate overnight in refrigerator.
2. Place chicken in your Instant Pot Mini, add oil and brown on all sides after pressing the 'Sauté' button.
3. Add coconut milk, spicy yellow curry powder, chopped dates, and cauliflower to the Instant Pot Mini.
4. Seal lid and cook after pressing 'Pressure Cook' on HIGH Pressure for 25 minutes. Please allow pressure to naturally release for about 20 minutes.
5. Place chicken and cauliflower on a serving tray or platter. Reduce the liquid in the IP Mini by pressing the 'Sauté' button, cook for 5 minutes or until thick enough.
6. Pour sauce over the serving platter with the chicken and cauliflower. If desired, garnish with jalapeños, and cilantro.

Nutritional (Per Serving)
Calories: 414
Fat: 29 g
Carbs: 10 g
Protein: 30 g

23. Instant Pot Mini Pork Ribs

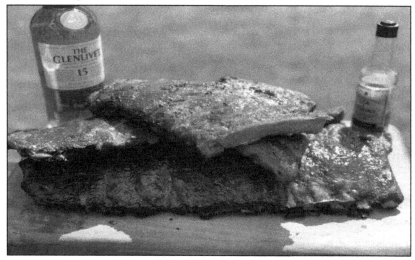

Serves: 3
Prep Time: 15 Minutes
Cook Time: 35 Minutes
Release Mode: Quick
Release Time: 10 Minutes

Ingredients
- 2.5 lbs. Pork ribs (cut into sections)
- 0.75 tbsp. salt
- 1.5 tbsp. Erythritol
- ¼ tsp., ground Black pepper
- ½ tsp., powder Garlic
- ½ tsp., powder Onion
- ½ tsp. Paprika
- ¼ tsp. Allspice
- ¼ tsp., ground Coriander
- ¼ cup Ketchup
- 1 tbsp. Red Wine Vinegar
- ¼ cup water (¼ cup)
- 1/8 tsp. Liquid smoke
- ¼ tbsp., ground Mustard
- ¼ tbsp., ground Allspice
- ¼ tsp. Onion powder
- 1/8 tsp. Xanthan gum

Directions

1. Set your Instant Pot Mini to sauté mode by pressing the 'Sauté' button and allow to heat up on high uncovered. Add your onions and garlic then allow to cook until soft (about 5 min).
2. Brown your ribs on top of the onions. When fully browned add in your remaining ingredients, except xanthan gum, and stir.
3. Close the lid and switch the setting on your Instant Pot Mini to the 'pressure mode by pressing the 'Pressure Cook' button and allow to cook on high for 35 minutes.
4. When the timer ends, do a quick release by carefully switching the pressure valve from 'sealed' to 'venting.'
5. This will allow your Instant Pot Mini to release the trapped pressure that is holding the cooker shut.
   Tip: Be extremely careful as you do this as the Instant Pot Mini will be hot, and the steam released can also burn your hands. Consider using an oven mitten or pot holder.
6. Carefully open, and stir in your xanthan gum, switch your cooker to the sauté setting and allow continue cooking for another 10 minutes.
7. Turn off your Instant Pot Mini, serve and enjoy!

Nutritional (Per Serving)
Calories: 337
Fat: 15.9 g
Carbs: 22.3 g
Protein: 25.9 g

24. Ropa Vieja

Serves: 3-4
Prep Time: 20 Minutes
Cook Time: 40 Minutes
Release Mode: Natural
Release Time: 20 Minutes

Ingredients
- ½ tbsp. Olive oil
- 1 lb. Beef flank steak
- Salt & pepper to taste
- ½ medium Onion (sliced)
- 2- 3 cloves Garlic (minced)
- ½ cup Chicken broth
    - oz Tomatoes (canned, diced)
- 1 cup Cubanelle peppers (sliced)
- ¼ tsp., dried Oregano
- ½ tsp., ground Cumin
- ½ Bay leaf
- ½ tsp. Goya Sazon
- ¼ cup Parsley (chopped, fresh)
- 1 tbsp. Vinegar
- ¼ cup Green Olives (chopped)

Directions
1. Set your Instant Pot Mini to sauté mode by pressing the 'Sauté' button and allow to heat up on high uncovered.
2. Add your onions and garlic then allow to cook until soft (about 5 min).
3. Season your steak with salt and pepper, then brown your steak on top of the onions.
4. When fully browned add in your remaining ingredients, except parsley, stir, and switch the setting on your Instant Pot Mini to the pressure setting by pressing the 'Pressure Cook' button and allow to cook on high for 40 minutes.
5. When the timer goes off, allow to cool down naturally for at least 20 minutes.
6. Carefully open and shred your steak. Discard your bay leaf from the remaining gravy, stir in your parsley, and return your pulled steak to the gravy.
7. Serve and enjoy!

Nutritional (Per Serving)
Calories: 325
Fat: 13.9 g
Carbs: 5.6 g
Protein: 43.2 g

25. Arroz Con Pollo

Serves: 4
Prep Time: 15 Minutes
Cook Time: 31 Minutes
Release Mode: Natural
Release Time: 20 Minutes

Ingredients
- 1.5 lbs. Chicken thighs (Boneless)
- 1.5 slices, sugar-free Bacon
- ½ sweet Onion
- ½ stalk dried herb blend Rhubarb (compliant Italian seasoning: oregano, thyme, rosemary)
- ½ tsp. Turmeric
- 1 bag, 6 oz of Frozen cauliflower rice
- ½ cup Bone broth

Optional:
- Steamed asparagus

Directions

1. Put IP Mini on sauté mode by pressing the 'Sauté' button. While pot heats, dice onion, garlic, bacon, and rhubarb. As soon as it reaches temperature add bacon and cook, occasionally stirring. Stir in bay leaves and diced vegetables.
2. Add skinned chicken thighs to pot once vegetables are cooked, stirring frequently until light brown in color.
3. Combine all seasoning, stirring thoroughly. Pour in vinegar and olive oil. Cover lid and set on "meat mode" by pressing the 'Meat/Stew' button and cooking for about 20 minutes with HIGH pressure.
4. Once meat has completed cooking, and the pressure has been released, it is now safe to open lid and mix in broth and cauliflower rice.
5. Seal the lid and cook on low for 3 mins. When the timer goes off, allow to cool down naturally for at least 20 minutes. Open the cover and mix well, breaking up chicken to have a shredded look.
6. If it is too fresh, adjust salt and serve!
7. Use steamed asparagus to garnish. Roasted bell pepper strips and peas are ideal and the traditional garnish for this dish.

Nutritional (Per Serving)

Calories: 196
Fat: 1 g
Carbs: 37 g
Protein: 11 g

26. Instant Pot Mini Chicken Curry

Serves: 3-4
Prep Time: 10 Minutes
Cook Time: 40 Minutes
Release Mode: Quick
Release Time: 10 Minutes

Ingredients
- ½ boneless and skinless chicken breasts, cut into cubes
- 3oz. can coconut milk
- 1garlic cloves, chopped
- 1/2 teaspoon fresh minced ginger
- 1/2 tomato, chopped
- 1/2 tablespoon curry powder
- 1/2 shallot, minced
- 1 tablespoons honey
- ¼ cup yogurt
- 3 dates, chopped
- 1 cups Cauli-Rice
- 1 ¼ cups water
- 1 pinch red pepper flakes
- Salt, to taste

Directions
1. In a bowl combine the yogurt, curry, honey, red pepper flakes, garlic, minced shallot and ginger in a blender.
2. Process until smooth. Place the remaining ingredients into your Instant Pot Mini and pour over the curry powder mix.
3. Close your lid and set to cook by pressing the 'Pressure Cook' button then set on HIGH pressure and allow to cook for about 1 hour.
4. When the timer ends, do a quick release by carefully switching the pressure valve from 'sealed' to 'venting.'
5. This will allow your Instant Pot Mini to release the trapped pressure that is holding the cooker shut.
   Tip: Be extremely careful as you do this as the Instant Pot Mini will be hot, and the steam released can also burn your hands. Consider using an oven mitten or pot holder.
6. Open, serve while still hot.

Nutritional (Per Serving)
Calories: 205
Fat: 12.3 g
Carbs: 3.1 g
Protein: 17.9 g

27. Shredded Chicken

Serves: 4
Prep Time: 5 Minutes
Cook Time: 20 Minutes
Release Mode: Quick
Release Time: 10 Minutes

Ingredients
- 4 lb. chicken breast
- ½ cup chicken broth
- 1 tsp. salt
- ½ tsp. black pepper

Directions
1. Put all the ingredients in the Instant Pot Mini. Cover Instant Pot Mini lid, check to ensure that the pressure valve is set to "sealed" and cook on HIGH pressure using the 'Pressure Cook' button for a period of 20 mins.
   Tip: As soon as cooking time is completed, cautiously turn the valve from "sealing" position to "venting" for quick pressure release. (This allows you to open the pot sooner than sitting around awaiting natural release).
2. Remove the chicken from pot onto a large plate, shred using two forks.
3. For storage, pack the chicken in a sealed container with the juice. The meet will be kept moist.

Nutritional (Per Serving)
Calories: 90.1
Fat: 2 g
Carbs: 1 g
Protein: 17 g

28. Asian Beef Pot Roast

Serves: 4
Prep Time: 5 Minutes
Cook Time: 35 Minutes
Release Mode: Quick
Release Time: 10 Minutes

Ingredients

For the pot roast:
- 5 lbs. Chuck roast (boneless)
- 3 cloves of Garlic (crushed)
- 2 tbsp. Ginger (peeled, chopped)
- 1 tsp. Orange (extract)
- ¼ cup Fish sauce
- 1 tsp., crushed Red pepper flakes
- ½ cup water
- 1 tbsp. Orange zest
- 1 tbsp. Stevia
- 1 tsp. Red wine vinegar

Recommended garnish options:
- 1 tsp. Orange zest (fresh)
- 1 tsp. Scallions (chopped)

For the Sriracha orange sauce:
- ¼ cup, sugar-free Mayonnaise
- 1 tsp. Sriracha hot sauce
- 1 tsp., granulated Sugar substitute
- ½ tsp., fresh Orange zest

Directions
1. Add all your pot roast ingredients into your Instant Pot Mini, stir, and close the lid.
2. Set to cook by pressing the 'Pressure Cook' button and cook on HIGH pressure for about 35 minutes.
3. When the timer ends, do a quick release by carefully switching the pressure valve from 'sealed' to 'venting.' This will allow your Instant Pot Mini to release the trapped pressure that is holding the cooker shut.
   Tip: Be extremely careful as you do this as the Instant Pot Mini will be hot, and the steam released can also burn your hands. Consider using an oven mitten or pot holder.
4. Carefully open, add your sauce ingredients, and stir. Garnish with your orange zest, and scallions. Enjoy.

Nutritional (Per Serving)
Calories: 245
Fat: 9.7 g
Carbs: 0 g
Protein: 38.3 g

29. Green Curry Cauliflower & Broccoli

Serves: 2
Prep Time: 15 Minutes
Cook Time: 5 Minutes
Release Mode: Natural
Release Time: 20 Minutes

Ingredients

For the marinade:
- ½ lbs. Broccoli (cut in florets)
- ¼ lbs. Cauliflower (cut in florets)
- ¼ tsp. Garlic powder
- ¼ tsp. Onion powder
- ¼ tbsp. Spicy green curry powder
- ½ tbsp. Olive oil
- ¼ tsp. Kosher salt

For the curry:
- ½ cups Coconut milk

- ¼ tbsp. Spicy green curry powder
- ¼ cup water
- 1/8 cup Chopped dates
- 1/8 cup Chopped cilantro (for garnish)
- 1/8 cup Fresh jalapeños (for garnish)

Directions
1. Wash and season broccoli, and cauliflower with marinade ingredients (except oil).
2. Leave to marinate overnight in refrigerator. Place broccoli and cauliflower in your Instant Pot Mini add oil and brown on all sides after pressing the 'Sauté' button. option.
3. Add coconut milk, spicy green curry powder, chopped dates, and cauliflower to the Instant Pot Mini.
4. Seal lid and cook after pressing the 'Pressure Cook' button on HIGH Pressure for 25 minutes.
5. Let pressure release naturally for about 20 minutes and remove top according to instructions from manufacturer.
6. Place broccoli, and cauliflower on a serving tray or platter.
7. Reduce the liquid in the pot by pressing the 'Sauté' button, cook for 5 minutes or until thick enough.
8. Pour sauce over the serving platter with the broccoli, and cauliflower.
9. If desired, garnish with jalapeños, and cilantro.

Nutritional (Per Serving)
Calories: 305.4
Fat: 8.6 g
Carbs: 4g
Protein: 5.4g

30. Pressure Cooker Pork and Kraut

Serves: 2-3
Prep Time: 10 Minutes
Cook Time: 40 Minutes
Release Mode: Natural & Quick
Release Time: 20 Minutes for Natural & 10 Minutes for Quick

Ingredients
- 1.5 lbs. Pork roast
- 1 tbsp. melted Coconut oil
- 1 large, sliced Onion
- 2 cloves Garlic (peeled, sliced)
- ½ cup water (filtered)
- Salt
- Black Pepper
- 2 cups Sauerkraut

Directions
1. Use your salt, and pepper to season your pork, and set aside. Place a skillet over high heat, add oil then add in your pork.
2. Allow your pork to brown on all sides. Fit your Instant Pot Mini with a rack and add your pork on top.
3. Add onion, water, and garlic. Season your pot again then close the lid, and make sure the pressure valve is set to "sealing."
4. Press the 'Pressure Cook' button and cook on HIGH pressure for 35 minutes.
5. When the timer ends, allow your pot to cool down naturally for about 20 minutes.
6. Open, and add a half of your sauerkraut. Return to pressure by pressing the 'Pressure Cook' button and set to cook on HIGH pressure for 5 minutes.
7. When the timer ends, do a quick release by carefully switching the pressure valve from 'sealed' to 'venting.'
   Tip: This will allow your Instant Pot Mini to release the trapped pressure that is holding the cooker shut. Be extremely careful as you do this as the Instant Pot Mini will be hot, and the steam released can also burn your hands. Consider using an oven mitten or pot holder.
8. Serve pork with raw, and cooked sauerkraut. Enjoy.

Nutritional (Per Serving)
Calories: 337
Fat: 12 g
Carbs: 6.2 g
Protein: 49.4 g

31. Pork Roast with Mushroom Gravy

Serves: 4
Prep Time: 15 Minutes
Cook Time: 1 Hour and 5 Minutes
Release Mode: Quick
Release Time: 10 Minutes

Ingredients
- 3 lbs. pork leg (1 piece)
- 1 tsp. sea salt
- ½ tsp. black pepper
- 4 cups of cauliflower (chopped)
- 1 med., diced onion
- 4 cloves garlic
- celery (2 ribs)
- ½ lb., sliced portabella mushrooms
- 6 tsp. organic coconut oil
- 2 cups filtered water

Directions

1. Place onion, cauliflower, celery, garlic and water at the bottom of the pressure cooker.
2. Now add pork leg seasoned with salt and pepper. Press the 'Pressure Cook' button and set to cook on HIGH pressure for 1½ hours if frozen and 1 hour if fully thawed.
3. Do a quick release by carefully switching the pressure vent from sealing to venting.
   Tip: This will allow your Instant Pot Mini to release the trapped pressure that is holding the cooker shut. Be extremely careful as you do this as the Instant Pot Mini will be hot, and the steam released can also burn your hands. Consider using an oven mitten or pot holder.
4. Remove pork from IP Mini gently and place it in a dish suitable for the oven.
5. Bake at 400 degrees in oven while making the gravy. This allows the fat to be rendered and enables the edges of the pork to be crisp and let it appears as it was slow roasted.
6. Take the vegetables already cooked along with broth and blend in a blender until smooth. Put aside until you are ready for it.
7. Ad your mushrooms to your IP Mini with your coconut oil by pressing the 'Sauté' button until soft (roughly 5 minutes).
8. Add to mixture the blended vegetables and continue cooking until gravy is thickened.
9. Serve gravy over sliced or shredded pork.

Nutritional (Per Serving)
Calories: 64
Fat: 0.4 g
Carbs: 14.2 g
Protein: 4 g

32. Belizean Stewed Chicken

Serves: 2
Prep Time: 10 Minutes
Cook Time: 25 Minutes
Release Mode: Natural
Release Time: 20 Minutes

Ingredients
- 4 pcs. Leg quarters
- 1 tbsp. coconut oil
- 2 tbsp. achiote seasoning/paste
- 2 tbsp. white vinegar
- 3 tbsp. Worcestershire sauce
- 1 cup sliced yellow onions
- 3 cloves, sliced garlic
- 1 tsp. ground cumin
- 1 tsp. dried oregano
- 1/2 tsp. ground black pepper
- 3 tsp. Keto granulated sugar substitute
- 2 cups chicken stock

Directions

1. Wash and section leg quarters (8 pcs). Mix together in a large container, Worcestershire sauce, achiote paste, cumin, sweetener, vinegar, oregano, and pepper. Mix thoroughly.
2. Add the pieces of chicken and rub the marinade in. Marinating time can start from one hour up.
3. Put the insert in the Instant Pot Mini and press the 'Sauté' button. Heat coconut oil and brown the chicken in sets, (don't throw away the marinade; keep for addition later).
4. Transfer seared chicken from Pot and put aside. Sauté onion slices and garlic in the Instant Pot Mini until softened.
5. Return the chicken parts to the Instant Pot Mini.
6. Throw out the chicken broth onto the leftover marinade and stir. Spread the marinade mixture over the chicken pieces in the Pot.
7. Set the Instant Pot Mini to cook by pressing the 'Pressure Cook' button on HIGH pressure and set for a 20 mins. period.
8. Let pressure release naturally for about 20 minutes and remove top according to instructions from manufacturer.
9. As soon as timer goes off, release steam. Check sauce if it has the desired taste. Serve hot, garnish with cilantro.

Nutritional (Per Serving)
Calories: 284
Fat: 16.8 g
Carbs: 28.7 g
Protein: 7.3 g

33. Dairy Free Beef Stroganoff

Serves: 2-3
Prep Time: 10 Minutes
Cook Time: 10 Minutes
Release Mode: None
Release Time: 0 Minutes

Ingredients
- ½ lb. Ground Beef
- 5 oz., frozen Shiitake mushrooms
- 1/2 cup (236mL) chicken broth
- ¼ red, chopped Onion
- ½ tsp., dried Parsley
- 1 tbsp. Vinegar (white wine)
- ½ tbsp. melted Coconut oil
- Salt to taste

Directions
1. Preheat your Instant Pot Mini by pressing the 'Sauté' button and add your coconut oil, and onions when hot.
2. Allow to cook until soft, and translucent. Add your ground beef, breaking it up as you add it on top of the onions.
3. Stir occasionally as you continue to cook, allowing it to brown fully.
4. Top with chicken broth, mushrooms, white wine vinegar, and parsley.

5. Leave to come to a boil on high. Adjust your Instant Pot Mini temperature to medium and maintain it at a good simmer uncovered.
6. Allow to cook, like this, for 4 minutes. Season to taste and serve over your spaghetti squash. Garnish with parsley. Enjoy!

Nutritional (Per Serving)
Calories: 34
Fat: 0.9 g
Carbs: 5 g
Protein: 2 g

34. Keto Instant Pot Mini Mexican Meatloaf

Serves: 2
Prep Time: 10 Minutes
Cook Time: 35 Minutes
Release Mode: Quick
Release Time: 10 Minutes

Ingredients:
- 2 lbs. ground beef
- 1 ¼ cup fire roasted salsa
- 1 tsp. cumin
- 1 tsp. garlic powder
- 1 tsp. chili powder
- 1 tsp. paprika
- 1 tsp. onion powder
- 1 tsp. sea salt
- 1 tsp. ground black pepper
- 1 large diced yellow onion
- 1 pastured egg
- ¼ cup Cassava flour
- 1 tsp. oil (ghee, avocado oil, or olive oil)

Directions
1. In the stainless-steel bowl within your Instant Pot Mini, pour the cup of water.
2. Mix all ingredients together in a bowl (saving ¼ cup of salsa) using clean hands.
3. Form meat mixture in a loaf, pressing it firmly together then wrapping it with aluminum foil then add it to the trivet.
4. Using a spoon, spread the remaining fire roasted salsa on top of the meatloaf. Seal the lid, press the 'Pressure Cook' button.
5. Use the +/- buttons to set the time to 35 minutes. Secure pressure valve; wait until completion of cook time, "quick releasing" the pressure valve.
6. After properly cooled, remove meatloaf with caution.
7. Serve. You can use fresh cilantro sprigs for garnishing and a drizzle of sauce of your choice to make it more delicious.

Nutritional (Per Serving)
Calories: 171
Fat: 6 g
Carbs: 9 g
Protein: 21.4 g

35. Instant Pot Mini No Noodle Lasagna

Serves: 4
Prep Time: 10 Minutes
Cook Time: 25 Minutes
Release Mode: Quick
Release Time: 10 Minutes

Ingredients
- ½ lb. Minced beef
- 2 cloves Garlic (minced)
- ½ small Onion (minced)
- 5/8 cups Ricotta cheese
- ¼ cup Parmesan cheese
- ½ large egg
- ½ jar, 12.5 oz. of Marinara sauce
- 4 oz. Sliced mozzarella

Directions:
1. Press the 'Sauté' button and allow your Instant Pot Mini to get hot. Season minced beef with onion and garlic and brown meat in your IP Mini.
2. While meat is being browned, combine in a small bowl the ricotta cheese, the Parmesan cheese, and egg.
3. Make sure to turn off sauté setting by pressing the 'Cancel' button when meat is done, especially if lasagna is being cooked in an Instant Pot Mini.
4. This prevents pot from being burnt at the bottom.
   Tip: Place a rack to cook lasagna in a pot which is covered inside of the "Instant Pot Mini," to prevent burning at the pot bottom.
5. Reserving half of the meat sauce, add sauce to meat after it completes browning.

6. Use half of the mozzarella cheese and top with some of the leftover sauce. On top of the mozzarella layer, spread half the ricotta cheese.
7. Top with the rest of meat sauce. Place another layer of mozzarella on top (reserving few slices for the last layer).
8. Use what is left of the ricotta cheese to spread over the mozzarella. Cover with the final slices of mozzarella.
9. Cover lasagna with a loose aluminum foil, this prevents condensation dripping on the cheese. This is not compulsory; it's not necessary if you want to add the top layer of cheese after the pressure cycle is finished.
10. Seal the lid, press the 'Pressure Cook' button and cook for 10 min on HIGH pressure.
11. Do a quick release then remove lid. Top with leftover cheese.
12. Sprinkle Parmesan cheese on top. If desired, cover and let stand to melt cheese. Scoop lasagna in bowls and serve.

Nutritional (Per Serving)
Calories: 365
Fat: 25 g
Carbs: 7 g
Protein: 25 g

36. Instant Pot Mini Chicken Tikka Masala

Serves: 4
Prep Time: 20 Minutes
Cook Time: 20 Minutes
Release Mode: Quick
Release Time: 10 Minutes

Ingredients
FOR MARINATING THE CHICKEN:
- 1 lb. Chicken breasts (boneless)
- 1 cup Greek yogurt (plain, 2% fat)
- 3 tsp. Garam masala
- 3 tsp. Lemon juice
- 1 tsp. Black pepper
- ¼ tsp. Ginger powder

FOR THE SAUCE:
- 1 tin, 15 oz. Tomato sauce
- 5 cloves Garlic (minced)
- 4 tsp. Garam masala
- ½ tsp. Paprika
- ½ tsp. Turmeric
- ½ tsp. Salt

- ¼ tsp. Cayenne pepper
- 1 cup Heavy whipping cream (to be added last)

Directions
1. Remove skin from chicken; wash and cut into 2-inch pieces.
2. Place marinade ingredients in a bowl (except chicken) and combine. Add pieces of chicken and rub in thoroughly with marinade.
3. Place aside, in the refrigerator and let stand for not less than 1 hour.
4. Press the 'Sauté' button on your IP Mini. When the temperature is reached, add chicken.
5. Sauté chicken until cooked, occasionally stirring; this should take about 6 min.
6. Set on HIGH pressure and combine all sauce ingredients (except whipped cream) over chicken and stir briskly.
7. Cover and seal lid. Press the 'Pressure Cook' button and cook with HIGH pressure for 10 min.
8. Release pressure using the quick release.
9. Return to sauté mode by pressing the 'Sauté' button then set to LOW.
10. When temperature is reached add whipped cream, mixing it with the other ingredients in the pot.
11. Simmer for a few minutes until sauce reaches desired consistency.
12. Serve and enjoy.

Nutritional (Per Serving)
Calories: 460
Fat: 27 g
Carbs: 19 g
Protein: 32 g

Instant Pot Meat & Poultry

37. Holiday Chicken in An Instant Pot Mini

Serves: 3
Prep Time: 5 Minutes
Cook Time: 20 Minutes
Release Mode: Natural
Release Time: 20 Minutes

Ingredients
- 2 lb. whole chicken (halved)
- choice seasonings
- ½ cup water
- 2 tsp. coconut oil

Directions
NB: Depending on the size of your chicken you may need to cook both halves in separate batches.
1. In an Instant Pot Mini, pour cup of water and place steam rack on the inside.
2. Heat oil in a large frying pot. Season chicken with seasonings and sear skin in oil for 60 sec. on each side, then remove frying pot from flame.
3. Put chicken on the steam rack in the Instant Pot Mini.
4. Close the lid in place on the Instant Pot Mini and ensure that the pressure vale is set to sealing. Press the 'Pressure Cook' button and set to HIGH pressure. Allow cooking time of 6 minutes for each pound of chicken.

5. When the time runs out, allow the Instant Pot Mini to cool down naturally for at least 20 minutes, then carefully open. Serve.
   Tip: You must always save your bones. Can be used to make broth to be used in other recipes.

Nutritional (Per Serving)
Calories: 107
Fat: 3 g
Carbs: 21 g
Protein: 1 g

38. Jamaican Jerk Pork Roast

Serves: 4
Prep Time: 10 Minutes
Cook Time: 10 Minutes
Release Mode: Natural
Release Time: 20 Minutes

Ingredients
- 4 lb. Pork shoulder
- ¼ cup, sugar-free Jamaican Jerk spice blend
- Salt
- Pepper
- 2 tbsp. Olive Oil
- 2 large Onions (finely minced)
- 4 cloves Garlic (minced)
- 1 cup water
- Plum Tomatoes, (2 (796ml) Cans, Italian, crushed)
- 2 Star Anise Pods
- 1 Bay Leaf

Directions
1. Trim and discard the excess fat from the top of the roast. Remove the excess liquid from it by patting it dry then proceed to season it with salt and pepper.
2. Press the 'Sauté' button, on medium setting heat the oil in your Instant Pot Mini.
3. Now, for 3 to 4 minutes per side char the pork, or char it until browned on every side, before transferring it off to a platter.
4. In the same oil, you browned the pork in, add your seasoning of onions and tomato paste, occasionally stirring for 10 minutes or until the onion gets very soft.
5. After this, garlic can be added while continuing to cooking for a minute or two.
6. Add red wine while stirring and watching for and putting back in any browned bits that are left in the pan.
7. Immediately after, add the crushed tomatoes and jerk spice.
8. Now, put back the roast into the pot and bring the mixture to a boil now by setting the Instant Pot Mini to high still on "sauté" mode.
9. The bay leaf and star anise should be wrapped in a cheesecloth pouch, dipped into the sauce and the pot covered.
10. With the pressure value set to "sealing," set the Instant Pot Mini to slow cook by pressing the 'Slow Cook' button and setting to HIGH pressure for 3 hours.
11. When the timer ends, click "cancel," and allow the pot to cool down naturally for about 20 minutes. Open, and discard the bay leaf and star anise. Serve hot.

Nutritional (Per Serving)
Calories: 282
Fat: 20 g
Carbs: 0 g
Protein: 23.1 g

39. Instant Pot Mini Stewed Pork

Serves: 3
Prep Time: 15 Minutes
Cook Time: 1 Hour and 30 Minutes
Release Mode: Natural
Release Time: 20 Minutes

Ingredients
- Thyme (1 sprig)
- Bay Leaf (1 dry)
- Cloves (1, whole)
- Cheesecloth
- Kitchen twine
- 1 lbs. Pork (trimmed, diced)
- ½ tsp. Sea salt
- ¼ tsp. Grounded black pepper
- ¼ cup Vegetable oil
- ½ Onion (small, diced)
- ½ Celery (stalk, diced)
- ½ tbsp. Tomato Paste
- ½ cup, dry White Wine
- 1.5 cups Pork Stock/Chicken Stock

- 1.5 tbsp. Parsley (chopped)
- ½ tbsp. Lemon Zest

Directions
1. Create a bouquet garni by tying your cheesecloth with the thyme, rosemary, cloves, and bay leaf cloves inside then secure it with a piece of twine.
2. Use a piece of paper towel to remove the excess moisture from the pork pieces in a patting motion. Season with salt and pepper.
3. Press the 'Sauté' button. Heat the oil in your Instant Pot Mini on "sauté" mode until it begins to smoke.
4. Set your pork to brown on all sides. Remove the pork pieces from the heat and set aside.
5. In your Instant Pot Mini, pour in the onion, and celery then add salt to season.
6. Sauté for about 8 minutes or until completely soft. Mix in the tomato paste to the onion mixture in the pot and add browned pork.
7. Pour in the white wine and allow it to cook until the liquid is reduced by half.
8. Pour in the 2 cups of the stock along with the bouquet garni and allow boiling.
9. Cover the pot, press the 'Meat/Stew' button and set to LOW pressure to simmer until the meat is literally falling off the bone when lifted for about an hour.
10. When the time ends allow the pressure to be released naturally for at least 20 minutes before opening.
11. When the meat has cooked remove the pork from the pot and plate in preparation to serve.
12. Remove and discard the kitchen twine and the bouquet garni. Use the juices from the pot to pour over the pork pieces.
13. Serve and enjoy!

Nutritional (Per Serving)
Calories: 198
Fat: 5 g
Carbs: 14 g
Protein: 28 g

40. Instant Pot Mini Spare Ribs

Serves: 2
Prep Time: 5 Minutes
Cook Time: 20 Minutes
Release Mode: Quick
Release Time: 10 Minutes

Ingredients
- 1 lb., spare ribs Pork
- 1 pk. Onion soup mix
- 1 bottle Buffalo sauce
- 1 cup water

Directions
1. Insert steam rack in Instant Pot Mini and add the cup of water. Sprinkle onion soup mix on both sides of pork ribs.
2. Place sprinkled pork on rack. Coat pork with buffalo sauce and save some for the topping.
3. Close your lid, press the 'Pressure Cook' button and set to HIGH pressure and allow to cook for about 20min.
4. When the timer ends, do a quick release by carefully switching the pressure valve from 'sealed' to 'venting.'

5. This will allow your Instant Pot Mini to release the trapped pressure that is holding the cooker shut.
   Tip: Be extremely careful as you do this as the Instant Pot Mini will be hot, and the steam released can also burn your hands. Consider using an oven mitten or pot holder.
6. Cautiously open, and top cooked pork ribs with remaining buffalo sauce. Enjoy!

Nutritional (Per Serving)
Calories: 277
Fat: 23 g
Carbs: 0 g
Protein: 15 g

41. Mexican Beef

Serves: 3
Prep Time: 15 Minutes
Cook Time: 45 Minutes
Release Mode: Natural
Release Time: 20 Minutes

Ingredients
- 1 ¼ lb. boneless beef
- ½ tbsp. chili powder
- 1 ½ tsp. kosher salt
- ½ tbsp. ghee
- ½ medium onion (thinly sliced)
- ½ tbsp. tomato paste
- 3 cloves garlic (peeled and crushed)
- ¼ cup roasted tomato salsa
- ¼ cup bone broth
- ¼ tsp. fish sauce
- ½ tsp. freshly ground black pepper
- ½ cup of cilantro (minced) (optional)
- 1 radish (thinly sliced) (optional)

Directions

1. Wash and cut beef into 2-inch pieces. Mix together in a large container, beef, salt and chili powder.
2. Add ghee to cooking insert on an Instant Pot Mini and press the 'Sauté' button. As soon as the ghee is melted, add sliced onions and sauté.
3. Onions should be translucent. Mix in garlic and tomato paste, cook until aromatic.
4. Put in seasoned beef; toss briefly. Add fish sauce, stock, and salsa. Follow these Directions: On the Instant Pot Mini, seal lid and push the 'Keep Warm' button.
5. Next, press the 'Meat/Stew' button to activate cooking mode. Set for 35 minutes, on HIGH pressure.
6. After the first 35 minutes press the 'Pressure Level' button and switch to LOW pressure.
7. When stew is finished, the cooker will adjust to the (Keep Warm) mode. Let pressure release naturally for at least 20 minutes.
8. Unlock lid and season with pepper and salt. When ready to serve, add the cilantro and radishes.
9. Stew can be refrigerated for 4-5 days, reheat before you serve. Enjoy

Nutritional (Per Serving)

Calories: 209
Fat: 13.4 g
Carbs: 7 g
Protein: 15 g

42. Pressure Cooker Pork Chops

Serves: 2-3
Prep Time: 10 Minutes
Cook Time: 20 Minutes
Release Mode: Quick
Release Time: 10 Minutes

Ingredients
- 2 Pork chops (boneless)
- 1 tbsp. Coconut oil (divided)
- ½ cup Chicken broth
- ½ Onion (sliced)
- 4 oz. chopped Mushrooms
- Salt & pepper to taste
- 1 tbsp. Butter

Directions
1. Set your Instant Pot Mini to preheat on "sauté" mode by pressing the 'Sauté' button. Season your pork chops with salt, and pepper.
2. Add in a tablespoon oil, then pork chops, and allow to brown on all sides for about 2 minutes per sides. Set aside.

3. Reheat on "sauté" mode. Add another tablespoon of oil to your Instant Pot Mini. Sauté your onions, and mushrooms until soft (about 2 minutes).
4. Add in your remaining ingredients, close your lid, and set your pressure valve to "sealing." Set on "pressure" mode by pressing the 'Pressure Cook' button, set on high, and allow to cook for about 10 minutes.
5. When the timer ends, do a quick release by carefully switching the pressure valve from 'sealed' to 'venting.'
   Tip: This will allow your Instant Pot Mini to release the trapped pressure that is holding the cooker shut. Be extremely careful as you do this as the Instant Pot Mini will be hot, and the steam released can also burn your hands.
6. Consider using an oven mitten or pot holder. Take out your pork chops, cover, and set aside.

Nutritional (Per Serving)
Calories: 231
Fat: 14 g
Carbs: 0.2 g
Protein: 24 g

43. Balsamic Chicken

Serves: 4
Prep Time: 10 Minutes
Cook Time: 20 Minutes
Release Mode: Quick
Release Time: 10 Minutes

Ingredients
- 4 6oz. skinless and boneless chicken breasts
- 8oz. quartered white mushrooms
- 4 tablespoons chopped parsley
- 2 shallots minced
- 1 teaspoon olive oil
- 1 ½ cups chicken stock
- ½ cup balsamic vinegar
- 2 tablespoons mustard
- 1 cup faro

Directions:
1. Combine the balsamic vinegar, chicken, and mustard in your Instant Pot Mini. Marinate for at least 30 minutes.
2. Discard the marinade. Set your Instant Pot Mini on "sauté" mode. Add oil and once hot add the shallots. Cook the shallots for 5 minutes.

3. Add the mushrooms and cook for 6-8 minutes or until the mushrooms have released juices. Stir in faro and cook for 3 minutes.
4. Stir in the stock and add the chicken.
5. Close your lid, and set your pressure set on HIGH, and allow to cook for about 1 hour.
6. When the timer ends, do a quick release by carefully switching the pressure valve from 'sealed' to 'venting.'
   Tip: This will allow your Instant Pot Mini to release the trapped pressure that is holding the cooker shut. Be extremely careful as you do this as the Instant Pot Mini will be hot, and the steam released can also burn your hands. Consider using an oven mitten or pot holder.
7. Serve the chicken while still hot with chicken and faro. Garnish with chopped parsley before serving.

Nutritional (Per Serving)
Calories: 107
Fat: 3 g
Carbs: 21 g
Protein: 1 g

44. Pressure Cooker Beef Short Ribs

Serves: 4
Prep Time: 10 Minutes
Cook Time: 1 Hour
Release Mode: Natural
Release Time: 20 Minutes

Ingredients
For short ribs:
- 4 Beef short ribs
- ¼ cup All-purpose flour
- 1 tsp. Salt
- ½ tsp. Black pepper
- 2 tbsp. Oil (alternatively use grapeseed, olive or canola oil)
- 1 medium sized onion (diced)
- 2 cloves Garlic (minced)
- 1 can, 12 oz. Tomato paste
- 2 cups Concord Grape wine
- 2-3 cups Beef broth
- Sage (2 sprigs)
- Thyme (2 sprigs)
- Rosemary (4 sprigs)

- 2 tsp. Cinnamon

For horseradish gremolata:
- ¼ cup Horseradish, shredded
- ½ cup Parsley (minced)
- Lemon zest (1 lemon)
- 1 tsp. Lemon juice
- 1 tbsp. Extra virgin olive oil
- Salt, to taste

Directions
1. Set your Instant Pot Mini on "sauté" mode to pre-heat. While its getting hot get your meat dipped into a flour, salt, and pepper mix.
2. Add in your oil in the Instant Pot Mini on high and brown all sides of your meat for about 10 minutes.
3. Set aside your meat now and remove all but a little of the fat so that you may be able to add in your onion to cook for 7 minutes until soft and brown.
4. Dropping your heat to medium add in your garlic and proceed to cook for 1 minute.
5. Increasing your heat back up to medium-high put in your tomato paste and cook for 5 minutes until the sauce becomes slightly brown.
6. Add wine to the pot and bring to a boil. Cook until the pot is reduced by half.
7. Place your meat back in and put in enough broth to almost cover the meat.
8. Now add your cinnamon and herbs. After the mixture is brought to boiling point, close your Instant Pot Mini lid, and make sure the pressure valve is set to sealing.
9. Switch your Instant Pot Mini to "meat" mode and allow to cook on high for 45 minutes.
10. When your timer ends, allow your pot to cool down naturally for at least 20 minutes before attempting to open it. We're almost done.
11. Open your pot, skim the fat from the sauce and strain the sauce after removing the meat.
12. Now for the gremolata: grate your horseradish after removing the skin, then combine with lemon juice, lemon zest, parsley, salt and olive oil.

Nutritional (Per Serving)
Calories: 471
Fat: 42 g
Carbs: 0 g
Protein: 22 g

45. Instant Pot Mini Pork Roast & Gravy

Serves: 3-4
Prep Time: 10 Minutes
Cook Time: 3 Hours and 30 Minutes
Release Mode: Natural
Release Time: 20 Minutes

Ingredients
- 2 lbs. Pork
- Salt
- Pepper
- 1 tbsp. Olive Oil
- 1 large Onion (finely minced)
- 1/8 cup Tomato Paste
- 2 cloves Garlic (minced)
- ½ cup dry Red Wine
- Plum Tomatoes, (1 (796ml) Cans, Italian, crushed)
- 1 Star Anise Pods
- 1 Bay Leaf
- Cooked Polenta
- Parmesan Cheese (Shredded)

Directions
1. Trim and discard the excess fat from the top of the roast. Remove the excess liquid from it by patting it dry then proceed to season it with salt and pepper.
2. On medium setting heat the oil in your Instant Pot Mini. Now, for 3 to 4 minutes per side char the pork, or char it until browned on every side, before transferring it off to a platter.
3. In the same oil, you browned the roast in, add your seasoning of onions and tomato paste, occasionally stirring for 10 minutes or until the onion gets very soft.
4. After this, garlic can be added while continuing to cooking for a minute or two.
5. Add red wine while stirring and watching for and putting back in any browned bits that are left in the pan.
6. Immediately after, add the crushed tomatoes and tomato juice. Now, put back the roast into the pot and bring the mixture to a boil now by setting the Instant Pot Mini to high still on "sauté" mode.
7. The bay leaf and star anise should be wrapped in a cheesecloth pouch, dipped into the sauce and the pot covered.
8. With the pressure value set to sealing, set the Instant Pot Mini to "slow cook" mode with high pressure. Set to cook on high for 3 hours.
9. When the timer ends, click "cancel," and allow the pot to cool down naturally for about 20 minutes.
10. Open, and discard the bay leaf and star anise. Remove your meat for cooling for about 5 minutes.
11. The pork can now be cut up into bite-sized pieces. Return the chopped pork to the pot and throw out any bone.
12. Dip your Ragu onto the pasta or polenta (these should be hot), and if needed, top with Parmesan cheese to serve.

Nutritional (Per Serving)
Calories: 34
Fat: 0.9 g
Carbs: 5 g
Protein: 2 g

46. Instant Pot Mini Boneless Pork Chops

Serves: 3
Prep Time: 5 Minutes
Cook Time: 5 Minutes
Release Mode: Quick
Release Time: 10 Minutes

Ingredients
- 3 pcs. Pork chops
- ½ tbsp. Coconut oil
- ½ stick of Butter
- ½ pack of Ranch mix
- ½ cup water or stock

Directions
1. In the Instant Pot Mini place pork chops and 1 tbsp. of coconut oil. Position setting to Sauté option and brown both sides.
2. It is not compulsory to brown them first, but it looks more presentable when you do so.
3. Spread the butter atop pork chops then sprinkle the packet of ranch mix. Pour cup of water or broth over pork.
4. Close your lid, and set your pressure set on high, and allow to cook for about 5 minutes.

5. When the timer ends, do a quick release by carefully switching the pressure valve from 'sealed' to 'venting.'
   Tip: This will allow your Instant Pot Mini to release the trapped pressure that is holding the cooker shut. Be extremely careful as you do this as the Instant Pot Mini will be hot, and the steam released can also burn your hands.
6. Consider using an oven mitten or pot holder. Serve.

Nutritional (Per Serving)
Calories: 202
Fat: 11 g
Carbs: 0.8 g
Protein: 25 g

47. Creamy Salsa Chicken

Serves: 3
Prep Time: 10 Minutes
Cook Time: 20 Minutes
Release Mode: Quick
Release Time: 10 Minutes

Ingredients
- 1.5 lbs. Chicken breasts
- ¼ cup Chicken broth
- 2 oz. Cream cheese
- ¼ cup Cottage cheese
- ½ cup Salsa
- ½ tsp. Taco or fajita seasoning

Directions
1. Place chicken breasts and broth in the Instant Pot Mini. Close your lid and set your Instant Pot Mini to 'Meat/Stew' on HIGH pressure and allow to cook for about 10 minutes.
2. When the timer ends, do a quick release by carefully switching the pressure valve from 'sealed' to 'venting.'
Tip: This will allow your Instant Pot Mini to release the trapped pressure that is holding the cooker shut. Be extremely careful as you do this as the Instant Pot Mini will be hot, and the steam released can also burn your hands. Consider using an oven mitten or pot holder.
3. Using a meat thermometer check if chicken is at least at a temperature of 160 degrees.
4. Place chicken into a large container. Save some of the liquid chicken was cooked in (1/2 cup) and throw away the rest.
5. Pour reserved cooking liquid into Instant Pot Mini, add the other ingredients and press 'sauté.'
6. Whisk contents until the cottage cheese and cream cheese melt. Turn valve to 'keep warm.'
7. Shred and add back the chicken to sauce in Instant Pot Mini. Serve.

Nutritional (Per Serving)
Calories: 529
Fat: 24 g
Carbs: 4 g
Protein: 71 g

Instant Pot Mini Soups & Stews

48. Instant Pot Mini Chili

Serves: 4
Prep Time: 15 Minutes
Cook Time: 52 Minutes
Release Mode: Natural
Release Time: 20 Minutes

Ingredients
- 2 ½ lbs. Ground Beef
- ½ large Onion (chopped)
- 8 Cloves (minced)
- 30 oz. Tomatoes (canned, diced, with liquid)
- 6 oz. Tomato paste
- 4 oz. Chilis (canned, green, with liquid)
- 2 tbsp. Worcestershire sauce
- ¼ cup Chili powder
- 2 tbsp. Cumin
- 1 tbsp. Dried oregano
- 2 tsp. Salt
- 1 tsp. Black pepper

Directions
1. Set your Instant Pot Mini to Sauté mode by pressing the 'Sauté' button and allow to heat up on high uncovered.
2. Add your onions and garlic then allow to cook until soft (about 5 min). Brown your beef on top of the onions.
3. When fully browned add in your remaining ingredients and stir.
4. Close the lid and switch the setting on your Instant Pot Mini to 'Pressure Cook' and allow to cook on High Pressure for 35 minutes.
5. Once the timer ends, allow to cool down naturally for about 20 minutes. Carefully open and enjoy!

Nutritional (Per Serving)
Calories: 306
Fat: 18 g
Carbs: 13 g
Protein: 23.3 g

49. Low Carb Goulash Soup

Serves: 3-4
Prep Time: 8 Minutes
Cook Time: 22 Minutes
Release Mode: Natural
Release Time: 20 Minutes

Ingredients
- 1 lbs. extra lean, ground Beef
- 1 tsp. Olive oil
- ½ Bell pepper (large, red, seeds removed and sliced)
- ½ large Onion (sliced)
- ½ tbsp. Garlic (minced)
- 1 tbsp. sweet Paprika
- ¼ tsp. Cayenne pepper
- 2 cups Beef stock
- Tomato (14.5 oz., diced)

Directions
1. Set your Instant Pot Mini to sauté mode by pressing the 'Sauté' button and allow to heat up on high uncovered.
2. Add your onions, paprika, and garlic then allow to cook until soft while stirring (about 5 min).
3. Season your beef with salt and pepper, then brown your beef on top of the onions until completely brown and broken apart.

4. Add in your remaining ingredients, stir, and switch the setting on your Instant Pot Mini to the 'Pressure Cook' setting with LOW pressure for 15 minutes.
5. When the timer goes off, allow to cool down naturally for about 20 minutes. Carefully open and enjoy!

Nutritional (Per Serving)
Calories: 383
Fat: 18.5 g
Carbs: 2.6 g
Protein: 44.5 g

50. Cabbage Soup

Serves: 2-3
Prep Time: 8 Minutes
Cook Time: 22 Minutes
Release Mode: Natural
Release Time: 20 Minutes

Ingredients
- 1 lbs. Ground Beef (90% lean)
- ¼ large Onion (diced)
- ½ clove Garlic (minced)
- ½ tsp. Ground cumin
- ½ large head, chopped Cabbage
- 2 cubes Bouillon
- ½ tin, 5 oz. Diced tomatoes
- ½ tin, 5 oz. Green chilies
- 2 cups water
- Salt and pepper (to taste)

Directions
1. Over medium flame, brown ground beef. Add and cook onions until they appear to be translucent.
2. Change over beef and onion mixture over to a stock pot. Add green chilies and diced tomatoes garlic, bouillon cubes, cumin, cabbage, and water to the pot.
3. Thoroughly mix ingredients, and over high flame bring to a boil.
4. Close your lid and set your Instant Pot Mini to 'Bean/Chili' on medium and allow to cook for about 45 minutes.
5. When the timer ends, do a quick release by carefully switching the pressure valve from 'sealed' to 'venting.'
   Tip: This will allow your Instant Pot Mini to release the trapped pressure that is holding the cooker shut. Be extremely careful as you do this as the Instant Pot Mini will be hot, and the steam released can also burn your hands. Consider using an oven mitten or pot holder.

Nutritional (Per Serving)
Calories: 261
Fat: 18 g
Carbs: 6 g
Protein: 17 g

51. Low-carb Loaded Cauliflower Soup

Serves: 4
Prep Time: 25 Minutes
Cook Time: 5 Minutes
Release Mode: Natural
Release Time: 20 Minutes

Ingredients

- 1 small Onion (diced)
- 2 tsp. Olive oil
- 1 large head Cauliflower (leaves and stem removed and the rest coarsely chopped)
- 3 cups Chicken stock (preferably homemade which should be more flavorful)
- 1 tsp. Garlic powder
- 1 tsp. Kosher salt
- ¼ cup Cream cheese (cut into cubes)
- 1 cup extra sharp cheddar cheese (grated)
- ½ cup Cream and milk (equal portions combined to make half and half)

TOPPING INGREDIENTS:
- extra sharp cheddar cheese
- sour cream
- bacon (10 strips, fried crisp and crumbled)
- thin slices of green onions

Directions
1. Peel onion, wash and diced into tiny pieces. Cut away leaves and most of the stem from cauliflower, letting the core remain. part.
2. Chop cauliflower into coarse pieces.
3. In your Instant Pot Mini, melt butter on Sauté mode. Following same, add onions and cook for 3 mins. Add chopped cauliflower, salt, chicken stock and garlic powder.
4. Close your lid, press the 'Pressure Cook' button and set your pressure set on HIGH, and allow to cook for about 1 hour.
5. When the timer ends, do a quick release by carefully switching the pressure valve from 'sealed' to 'venting.'
6. **Tip:** This will allow your Instant Pot Mini to release the trapped pressure that is holding the cooker shut. Be extremely careful as you do this as the Instant Pot Mini will be hot, and the steam released can also burn your hands. Consider using an oven mitten or pot holder.
7. During the cooking of the soup, prepare creamed cheese cubes, grated extra sharp cheddar, cream and milk (combined, is called half and half).
8. Cook bacon; crumble (you can use pre-cooked bacon and crisp it in the microwave to lessen extra fat).
9. In a dish, prepare topping with sour cream and extra grated cheese then add slices of green onions. Set aside until you are ready for it.
10. Check pot to see if cauliflower is cooked; place Instant Pot Mini on KEEP WARM (if using a pressure cooker select simmer or low).
11. Puree soup with an immersion blender, blender, or a food processor. (It is better to use an immersion blender to puree the soup in a pressure cooker. Not to worry if you don't have one).
12. Check consistency of soup, and if it is not to your suit, you can add some more stock to make it thinner and if it is too thin simmer some more.
13. Melt together grated cheese, and cubed cream cheese add to puree and stir gently.
14. Stir in cream and milk mixture (half and half), continue heating; season with black pepper and salt to desired taste.

15. Serve hot, place topping consisting of crumbled bacon, grated cheese, sour cream, and green onion on the table to add to soup at the table.

Nutritional (Per Serving)
Calories: 105
Fat: 8 g
Carbs: 6 g
Protein: 4 g

52. IP Mini Pulled Pork Chili

Serves: 4
Prep Time: 10 Minutes
Cook Time: 5 Minutes
Release Mode: Natural
Release Time: 20 Minutes

Ingredients
- 2 lbs. pork roast
- 3 cloves garlic (peeled)
- ½ cup hot sauce
- 3 tbsp. paprika (smoked)
- 2 tbsp. garlic powder
- 2 tbsp. chili powder
- 1 tbsp. cumin
- 2 tsp. cayenne pepper
- 1 tbsp. red pepper flakes
- 1 -2 tsp. salt (depending on taste)
- 2 cloves, diced onions
- 1 diced red bell pepper
- 1 diced yellow bell pepper
- 2, 14 oz. fire roasted tomatoes
- 1, 14 oz. tomato sauce

- avocado slices (to garnish)
- green onions (diced for garnishing)

Directions
1. Put pork roast in an Instant Pot Mini. Pierce three holes with knife into roast and insert cloves of garlic. Cover meat with hot sauce. Sprinkle the cayenne pepper, cumin, garlic powder, chili powder, salt and flakes of red pepper, at the top of roast.
2. Place tomatoes, bell pepper, diced onions and tomato sauce on top of the roast.
3. Cover lid, and set the pressure valve to "Sealing," cook for 9-10 hours on the "low."
4. When the timer ends, allow to cool naturally for about 20 minutes before trying to open the lid.
5. Open carefully, serve, and use sliced avocado and diced green onions for garnishing. Enjoy.

Nutritional (Per Serving)
Calories: 360
Fat: 20 g
Carbs: 22 g
Protein: 21.2 g

53. Chickpea Soup

Serves: 2-3
Prep Time: 10 Minutes
Cook Time: 9 Minutes
Release Mode: Quick
Release Time: 10 Minutes

Ingredients
- 7.5oz. can chickpeas, dry, soaked
- 1 zucchinis, trimmed, cubed
- 1 sprigs thyme
- 1/2 leek, white and light green parts chopped
- ¼ cup bulgur
- 2oz. green beans, cut into ½-inch pieces
- 2 cups water
- 1 garlic cloves, minced
- 1 cups chicken stock
- 1.5 tablespoons butter
- 1/2 cup tomatoes, chopped
- 1/2 jalapeno, seeded and chopped
- 1/2 cup fresh peas
- 1/2 bay leaf
- Salt and pepper, to taste

Directions:
1. Set your Instant Pot Mini to "rice" mode and allow to preheat. When hot add butter and leave to melt.
2. Add celery, chickpeas, leek, garlic, zucchinis, garlic, and jalapeno.
3. Cook, stirring for 4 minutes.
4. Add the stock, bulgur, tomatoes, bay leaf, water, and thyme. Close your lid, and set your pressure set on high, and allow to cook for about 10 minutes.
5. When the timer ends, do a quick release by carefully switching the pressure valve from 'sealed' to 'venting.'
   Tip: This will allow your Instant Pot Mini to release the trapped pressure that is holding the cooker shut. Be extremely careful as you do this as the Instant Pot Mini will be hot, and the steam released can also burn your hands. Consider using an oven mitten or pot holder.
6. Open, add the green beans and peas. Discard the thyme., reheat on "sauté" mode and allow to cook for 5 more minutes. Serve.

Nutritional (Per Serving)
Calories: 113
Fat: 2 g
Carbs: 26 g
Protein: 9 g

54. Zuppa Toscana

Serves: 3
Prep Time: 10 Minutes
Cook Time: 4 Hours and 10 Minutes
Release Mode: Natural
Release Time: 20 Minutes

Ingredients
- 1 tbsp. olive oil
- ½ Onion (chopped, yellow)
- 2 cloves garlic (minced)
- ½ lb. Italian Sausage (turkey/ chicken)
- 2.5 cups chicken broth
- 1 tsp., dried basil
- ½ tsp. dried fennel
- 1 cup of chopped kale
- ¼ cup heavy cream
- ½ tbsp., crushed red pepper
- salt and pepper to taste

Directions
1. In a suitable sized skillet, preheat and add your preferred cooking oil; place garlic, onion, and sausage.
2. Cook for a minimum of 5 minutes (meat does not have to be fully cooked). Drain grease and add the sausage mixture to the Instant Pot Mini.
3. Place Chicken broth, and herbs atop sausage. Turn cooker on low for four hours using the 'Slow Cook' setting.
4. When the timer ends, allow to naturally cool down for about 20 minutes, before trying to open the lid.
5. Carefully open, and add the kale, secure the lid and restart for another half an hour.
6. Cool naturally once more, then add your cream, salt, red pepper (crushed) and enjoy.

Nutritional (Per Serving)
Calories: 170
Fat: 4 g
Carbs: 24 g
Protein: 10 g

55. Chicken Chili Verde

Serves: 3-4
Prep Time: 10 Minutes
Cook Time: 6 Minutes
Release Mode: Quick
Release Time: 10 Minutes

Ingredients
- 3 lbs. chicken leg and thigh
- ¾ lb. tomatillos (discard husk, section in quarters)
- 1 lb. poblano peppers (chopped without seeds and stem)
- 5 oz. Cubanelle peppers (chopped, without seeds and stem)
- 2 whole jalapeño chilies (chopped without stem)
- 10 oz. chopped white onion
- 6 cloves garlic
- 4 tsp. whole cumin seed (toasted and ground)
- Kosher salt
- fresh cilantro leaves (3/4 cup – including some for garnish)
- fish sauce (Asian, 1 tbsp.)
- For serving, use crispy corn tortillas and lime slices.

Directions

1. In an Instant Pot Mini, combine all peppers, chicken, tomatillos, onion, garlic, cumin, and a 1/2 tsp. of salt.
2. Press the 'Sauté' button and set to HIGH until light sizzle is visible. Seal Instant Pot Mini.
3. When it develops a high pressure, cook for 15 minutes then do a quick release.
4. Place chicken pieces in a container and set aside. Add fish sauce, and 1/2 cup of cilantro leaves to the mixture in the Instant Pot Mini.
5. Use a hand or standing blender to combine mixture and season with salt to desired taste.
6. Remove skin and bones from chicken and return it to the sauce.
7. Serve on a platter, decorated with chopped cilantro. Serve warm with tortillas and lime slices.

Nutritional (Per Serving)
Calories: 140
Fat: 2.2 g
Carbs: 7.4 g
Protein: 19.5 g

56. Pressure-Cooked Lamb Stew

Serves: 2-3
Prep Time: 5 Minutes
Cook Time: 35 Minutes
Release Mode: Quick
Release Time: 10 Minutes

Ingredients

- 1 lbs. Lamb stew meat
- ½ Acorn squash
- ½ large, yellow Onion (sliced)
- Rosemary (1/2 sprig)
- 1 Bay leaf
- 3 cloves Garlic (sliced)
- 1.5 tbsp. Vegetable broth
- 1/8 tsp. Salt (to taste)
- ½ tbsp. Ghee

Directions

1. Wash and cut lamb into 2-inch pieces. Mix together in a large container, lamb, and salt. Add ghee to cooking insert on an Instant Pot Mini and press "sauté."
2. As soon as the ghee is melted, add sliced onions then sauté. Onions should be translucent.
3. Mix in garlic, cook until aromatic.
4. Put in seasoned lamb; toss briefly. Add in your remaining ingredients and stir. Close your lid and set your pressure valve to "sealing." Set on "Pressure Cook" mode, set on high, and allow to cook for about 10 minutes.
5. When the timer ends, do a quick release by carefully switching the pressure valve from 'sealed' to 'venting.'
6. **Tip:** This will allow your Instant Pot Mini to release the trapped pressure that is holding the cooker shut. Be extremely careful as you do this as the Instant Pot Mini will be hot, and the steam released can also burn your hands. Consider using an oven mitten or pot holder. Enjoy!

Nutritional (Per Serving)

Calories: 253
Fat: 11 g
Carbs: 12 g
Protein: 26 g

57. Spicy Brazilian Fish Stew

Serves: 2
Prep Time: 10 Minutes
Cook Time: 15 Minutes
Release Mode: Quick
Release Time: 10 Minutes

Ingredients
- 1 lb. White fish (wild caught)
- 1 medium Lime (juiced)
- 1 medium Jalapeno pepper (seeds removed)
- 1 medium Onion (sliced)
- 1 medium Red pepper
- 1 medium Yellow pepper
- 2 cloves Garlic (minced)
- 1 tsp. Paprika
- Tomatoes (2 cups, chopped)

- Salt (1 tsp.)
- Black Pepper (¼ tsp.)
- Coconut milk (15 oz., organic)

Optional garnishes
- Cilantro (1 tsp., chopped, fresh)

Directions
1. Add your lime juice, and fish in a mixing bowl, and set aside to marinate. Set your Instant Pot Mini to preheat on "sauté" mode.
2. Add in oil, onions, and peppers then continue to sauté, while stirring, until the onions are soft. Add garlic then cook for 30 seconds.
3. Add the white fish and chopped tomatoes to the pot. Pour the coconut milk over the mixture.
4. Close your lid and set your pressure valve to "sealing." Set on "Pressure Cook" mode, set on high, and allow to cook for about 10 minutes.
5. When the timer ends, do a quick release by carefully switching the pressure valve from 'sealed' to 'venting.'
   Tip: This will allow your Instant Pot Mini to release the trapped pressure that is holding the cooker shut. Be extremely careful as you do this as the Instant Pot Mini will be hot, and the steam released can also burn your hands. Consider using an oven mitten or pot holder.
6. Open, top with chopped cilantro. Enjoy.

Nutritional (Per Serving)
Calories: 373
Fat: 30 g
Carbs: 10 g
Protein: 20 g

58. Chicken Faux Pho

Serves: 4
Prep Time: 10 Minutes
Cook Time: 42 Minutes
Release Mode: Natural
Release Time: 20 Minutes

Ingredients
- 4 lbs. assorted chicken pieces
- 2 cloves onions
- 1-inch ginger (peeled and roughly chopped)
- 1 tbsp. coriander seed
- 1 tsp., green cardamom pods
- 1, black cardamom pod
- 1 cinnamon stick
- 4 Cloves
- 1 stalk of lemon grass (cut in 2-inch pieces)
- ¼ fish sauce
- 1 cup Cilantro
- 1 head, roughly chopped Bok choy
- 1, spiralized daikon root
- salt to taste

<u>For Garnish</u>
- lime (2 wedges)
- basil (1 cup)
- mung bean sprouts
- jalapenos (2, thinly sliced)
- Onion (¼, thinly sliced)

Directions
1. In a dry skillet add the coriander seeds preheat at medium low heat until they start to become slightly and slighter brown.
2. Wash chicken pieces and place in pressure cooker; now add the cilantro, lemon grass, onions, fish sauce and dry spices.
3. Pour cold water to cover. Close the lid. Press the 'Pressure Cook' button. Set the timer for 30 minutes on HIGH pressure.
4. When the timer is up, allow to naturally cool down for about 20 minutes and set the chicken pieces to cool until ready to be served.
5. Strain broth and put it back to pressure. Add salt for flavor. Allow pot to simmer, while simmering add the spiralized daikon and Bok choy. Cook until meat is tender.
6. Place chicken and noodles into separate bowls and spoon in the broth. Serve with the garnishes and enjoy!

Nutritional (Per Serving)
Calories: 350
Fat: 20.4 g
Carbs: 50 g
Protein: 21 g

59. Instant Pot Mini Chicken Soup with Kale

Serves: 4
Prep Time: 10 Minutes
Cook Time: 15 Minutes
Release Mode: Quick
Release Time: 10 Minutes

Ingredients
- 2 tbsp. butter
- 1 finely, chopped onion
- 4 stalks, chunked celery
- 2 cups bay leaves
- 1 -2 tsp. salt
- ½ tsp. black pepper
- ½ tsp., dried thyme
- ¼ tsp., dried oregano
- 4 cups chicken broth
- 1 lb. shredded chicken/ breast

- 2 cups chopped kale
- ½ tsp. Fish sauce

Directions
1. On the Instant Pot Mini select the Sauté Button then add the onions and butter.
2. Sauté until tender, for a minimum of 5 minutes, then add the celery, bay leaves, pepper, salt, thyme, and oregano.
3. Sauté until distinct, for approximately 1 minute, then apply the chicken broth and water to fill the "6 cup" line in the Instant Pot Mini.
4. Secure the pot and select the "Keep Warm/Cancel" option to cancel the Sauté function, then adjust pot to the "Soup/Broth" option and set for a minimum of 4 mins on (HIGH pressure).
5. When finished do a quick release method the steam. After the steam has escaped detach the lid, then add kale and chicken.
6. Let the soup set for 60 secs until kale begins to turn bright green. Add fish sauce, salt and pepper and Stir. Taste, then serve. Enjoy!

Nutritional (Per Serving)
Calories: 120
Fat: 3 g
Carbs: 13 g
Protein: 7 g

60. Beef Brisket Pho

Serves: 4
Prep Time: 20 Minutes
Cook Time: 40 Minutes
Release Mode: Natural
Release Time: 20 Minutes

Ingredients
- 1 lbs. Brisket
- ½ lb. Beef soup bones
- Dry shiitake beef mushrooms (5/8 cup, rehydrate in room temperature water overnight)
- Yellow onion (1.5 medium, peeled and leave as a whole)
- Leek (1.5 large size, roughly diced into segments
- Water
- 1 ¼ tsp. Fine sea salt
- 1.5 tsp. Red boat fish sauce
- Cheese cloth

<u>*Pho Aroma Combo:*</u>
- ginger (1 fat joints, scrub clean)
- 2 anise (star)
- 1 cinnamon stick

- 4 green cardamom
- 1 ½ medium size shallots
- 2.5 cilantro roots

Garnish:
- Lime wedges
- Baby bok choy
- Bean sprouts
- Red or green Fresno chili peppers
- Mint leaves
- Asian/Thai basil (optional)
- Cilantro (optional)
- Hot chili pepper sauce (optional)

Directions

Pre-Cooking:
1. Soak dry mushrooms in room temperature water overnight. If pressed for time, soak mushrooms in warm water until the mushrooms are tender.
2. Pre-boil soup bones and briskets: add the bones and brisket to a large suitable pot covered with water.
3. Over high flame bring water to a boil, then lower flame and simmer for 10 mins.
4. Rinse bones and meat under tap water (room temperature). Put aside. Throw away the broth.
5. Put 'Pho Aroma Combo' ingredients together and grill over medium heat. Shake and stir ingredients until a nice fragrance emanate.
6. Try not to spoil aroma by burning combination. Chop leeks, and mushrooms (save water from mushroom).
7. Place leeks and aroma combo in a large cheesecloth and tie it with a string.

Instant Pot Mini Cooking:
8. In a large Instant Pot Mini, place beef bones and brisket (fat side up), aroma combination and leeks (in cheese cloth).
9. Add strained mushroom water to the pot. Pour more water in the pot until it is at the 4-liter mark.
10. Seal the lid, press "Soup/Broth" and adjust time to 40 minutes/HIGH pressure.
11. Let Instant Pot Mini release naturally for about 20 minutes, throw away aroma combination bag.
12. Remove the beef brisket; soak it in cold water for at least 9 minutes (this prevents brisket from turning dark in color).

13. Throw away aroma bags, beef bones, and yellow onion. Season broth with fine sea salt, and fish sauce.
14. Thin slice beef brisket in thin slices at 45- degree angle against the grain.
15. Spoon the broth over sliced beef brisket, mint leaves, chili peppers, bean sprouts, mushrooms, and Asian basil. Serve hot, garnish with lime wedges.

Nutritional (Per Serving)
Calories: 348
Fat: 7.1 g
Carbs: 34 g
Protein: 42 g

61. Split Asparagus Soup

Serves: 3
Prep Time: 15 Minutes
Cook Time: 15 Minutes
Release Mode: Quick
Release Time: 10 Minutes

Ingredients
- 1 lb. split asparagus
- 1 ½ tbsp. ghee
- 3 cloves garlic (pressed)
- ½ white, diced onion
- ½ chopped ham bone
- 2 cups chicken broth
- ¼ tsp. dried thyme
- salt and pepper to taste

Directions
1. On the Instant Pot Mini select the Sauté option and allow ghee to melt.
2. Place the diced onions in the Instant Pot Mini and Sauté for 5 minutes, until it becomes brown.
3. Add the ham bone, pressed garlic, and broth, and bring to a simmer for 3 mins.
4. Place the asparagus and the thyme and secure the Instant Pot Mini.

5. Adjust to the Soup/Broth setting and set the time for a minimum of 45 minutes.
6. When the timer ends, do a quick release by carefully switching the pressure valve from 'sealed' to 'venting.'
   Tip: This will allow your Instant Pot Mini to release the trapped pressure that is holding the cooker shut. Be extremely careful as you do this as the Instant Pot Mini will be hot, and the steam released can also burn your hands. Consider using an oven mitten or pot holder.
7. Blend with a food processor and serve!

Nutritional (Per Serving)
Calories: 65
Fat: 3.3 g
Carbs: 7 g
Protein: 2.6 g

62. Pork Cheek Stew

Serves: 2
Prep Time: 10 Minutes
Cook Time: 25 Minutes
Release Mode: Quick
Release Time: 10 Minutes

Ingredients
- 1 lb. Pork cheek
- 1 tbsp. coconut oil
- 2 tbsp. achiote seasoning/paste
- 2 tbsp. white vinegar
- 3 tbsp. Worcestershire sauce
- 1 cup sliced yellow onions
- 3 cloves garlic, (sliced)
- 1 tsp. ground cumin
- 1 tsp. dried oregano
- 1/2 tsp. ground black pepper
- 3 tsp. granulated sugar substitute
- 2 cups pork stock

Directions

1. Wash and dry pork cheeks. Mix together in a large container, Worcestershire sauce, achiote paste, cumin, sweetener, vinegar, oregano, and pepper.
2. Mix thoroughly.
3. Add the pieces of chicken and rub the marinade in. Marinating time can start from one hour up.
4. Put the insert in the Instant Pot Mini and set setting to 'Sauté.'
5. Heat coconut oil and brown the pork cheeks in sets, (don't throw away the marinade; keep for addition later).
6. Transfer seared chicken from Pot and put aside. Sauté onion slices and garlic in the Instant Pot Mini until softened.
7. Return the pork cheeks to the Instant Pot Mini.
8. Throw out the pork broth onto the leftover marinade and stir. Spread the marinade mixture over the pork cheeks in the pot.
9. Follow the manufacturer's instruction in sealing the Instant Pot Mini. Set the Instant Pot Mini to 'Pressure Cook'," "HIGH pressure," and set for a 20 mins. period.
10. Let the Instant Pot Mini release naturally for about 20 minutes Check sauce if it has the desired taste. Serve hot, garnish with cilantro.

Nutritional (Per Serving)

Calories: 337
Fat: 12 g
Carbs: 6.2 g
Protein: 49.4 g

63. Quick Onion Soup

Serves: 4
Prep Time: 10 Minutes
Cook Time: 25 Minutes
Release Mode: Quick
Release Time: 10 Minutes

Ingredients
- 2 tbsp. avocado oil /coconut oil
- 3 medium, yellow onions
- 1 tbsp. balsamic vinegar
- 6 cups pork stock
- 1 tsp. salt
- 2 cups bay leaves
- thyme (2 sprigs)

Directions
1. Peel and slice onions in halves and cut into thin moons. Adjust Instant Pot Mini to Sauté option and add the preferred oil.
2. Once oil becomes hot add the onions. Sauté until onions become translucent and pale. Stir often to prevent onions from sticking, it should take about 15 mins.
3. Scrape the remains from the bottom of the pot then sprinkle the balsamic vinegar in the pot while adding the salt, bay leaves, and thyme.

4. Turn off the Instant Pot Mini, secure the lid and ensure that the vent isn't blocked, and lid is set in the Sealing Position.
5. Set Pot to the "HIGH Pressure" option and cook the soup for 10 mins. Release pressure using the quick release option on the Instant Pot Mini.
6. Remove sprigs of thyme and bay leaves from pot and blend soup using an electric blender or an Immersion blender.

Nutritional (Per Serving)
Calories: 23
Fat: 0.7 g
Carbs: 3.3 g
Protein: 1.7 g

64. Instant Pot Mini Beef Curry Stew

Serves: 2-3
Prep Time: 5 Minutes
Cook Time: 50 Minutes
Release Mode: Natural
Release Time: 20 Minutes

Ingredients
- 1 ¼ lb. Beef stew
- ½ lb. Broccoli florets
- 1 ½ chopped Zucchinis
- ¼ cup Chicken broth
- 1 tbsp. Curry powder
- ½ tbsp. Garlic powder
- Salt to taste
- 7 oz. Coconut milk

Directions
1. Set your Instant Pot Mini to "sauté" mode by pressing the 'Sauté' button and allow to get hot.
2. Once hot add in your beef stew and top with your powdered seasonings.

3. Allow to cook for about 5 minutes, while stirring, allowing the beef stew to brown. Add your remaining ingredients into the Instant Pot Mini and mix to combine.
4. Close your lid and set the pressure valve to sealing. Press the 'Pressure Cook' button to cook on high pressure for 45 minutes.
5. When the timer ends, allow to cool down naturally for about 15 minutes before trying to open.
6. Cautiously open and add your coconut milk. Stir, then adjust the seasoning to your preference. Serve.

Nutritional (Per Serving)
Calories: 490
Fat: 30 g
Carbs: 8 g
Protein: 40 g

65. Low Carb Bone Broth

Serves: 3
Prep Time: 10 Minutes
Cook Time: 1 Hour
Release Mode: Natural
Release Time: 20 Minutes

Ingredients
- 1 chicken carcass (whole chicken with majority flesh removed) & any drippings
- 1-inch ginger
- 1 onion (small cut in quarters with skin on)
- 1 cup celery tops (chopped)
- 2 cloves garlic
- 6 tsp. apple cider vinegar
- 4 quarts filtered water

Directions
1. Pour in filtered water until it reaches the 2-quart mark then add in all your ingredients. Seal Instant Pot Mini according to manufacturer's instructions.
2. Press the 'Pressure Cook' button and set to cook on HIGH pressure for 60 minutes.

3. When the time is up, release the pressure from pot naturally for about 20 minutes.
4. Carefully open and allow to cool for about one hour. Strain out all the solids into a clean large enough container.
5. Season broth with sea salt to taste. Allow to stand in refrigerator for several hours.
6. Discard solidified fat which formed at the top of the broth.
7. Packaged and store into containers up to one week in the refrigerator, or frozen for up to 12 weeks.

Nutrition (Per Serving)
Calories: 64
Fat: 0.4 g
Carbs: 14.2 g
Protein: 4 g

66. Tomatillo Chili

Serves: 4
Prep Time: 15 Minutes
Cook Time: 35 Minutes
Release Mode: Naturally
Release Time: 20 minutes

Ingredients
- ½ lb., ground Beef
- ½ lb., ground Pork
- Tomatillos (1.5, chopped)
- Onion (¼ white, chopped)
- 3 oz. Tomato paste
- ½ tsp. Garlic Powder
- ½ Jalapeno Pepper (chopped, including seeds)
- ½ tbsp. ground Cumin
- ½ tbsp. Chili Powder
- Salt (to taste)

Directions
1. Set your Instant Pot Mini by pressing the 'Sauté' button.
2. Once hot, add in your ground pork, and beef and cook until fully browned, while stirring.
3. Next add your water, chili powder, cumin, jalapeno, tomato paste, garlic, onion, tomatillo. Stir to combine.
4. Close the lid, and make sure that your pressure valve is set to sealing.
5. Set the Instant Pot Mini to cook by pressing the 'Pressure Cook' button on HIGH pressure for about 35 minutes.
6. When the timer ends, allow the Instant Pot Mini to cool down naturally for at least 20 minutes before trying to open. Serve.

Nutritional Information per Serving:
Calories: 325; Total Fat: 23 g; Carbs: 6 g; Dietary Fiber: 1 g; Sugars: 3 g; Protein: 20 g; Cholesterol: 81 mg; Sodium: 256 mg

67. Broccoli Cheese Soup

Serves: 4
Prep Time: 15 Minutes
Cook Time: 5 Minutes
Release Mode: Quick
Release Time: 10 minutes

Ingredients
- 2 tbsp. Butter
- 1 tbsp. Onion powder
- Broccoli (1 large bunch, cut off florets and discard stems)
- 4 cups Chicken stock
- ¼ tsp. Garlic powder
- 1 cup Heavy cream
- 2 cups Sharp cheddar cheese
- 1 tsp. Salt
- 1 tsp. Pepper

Directions
1. Remove lid from Instant Pot Mini. Press the 'Sauté' button and add butter. Heat butter to high until it is sizzling.
2. Add broccoli florets, chicken stock, pepper and salt, garlic and onion powder
3. Close your lid, press the 'Pressure Cook' button and set to cook for about 5 minutes on HIGH pressure.
4. When the timer ends, do a quick release by carefully switching the pressure valve from 'sealed' to 'venting.' This will allow your Instant Pot Mini to release the trapped pressure that is holding the cooker shut.
   TIP: Be extremely careful as you do this as the Instant Pot Mini will be hot, and the steam released can also burn your hands. Consider using an oven mitten or pot holder.
5. Stir in cheddar cheese and heavy cream. Enjoy!

Nutrition (Per Serving)
Calories: 190
Fat: 11 g
Carbs: 16 g
Protein: 6 g

Instant Pot Dessert Recipes

68. Instant Pot Mini Keto Chocolate Mini Cakes

Serves: 2
Prep Time: 10 Minutes
Cook Time: 25 Minutes
Release Mode: Quick
Release Time: 10 minutes

Ingredients
- 2 tbsp. Splenda
- 2 large eggs
- 2 tbsp. Heavy cream
- ½ tsp. Baking powder
- 1 tsp. Vanilla extract
- ¼ cup Baking cocoa

Directions
1. Combine dry ingredients in a container. Add heavy cream, vanilla extract, and eggs. Whisk until smooth. Grease ramekins and fill each cup half way.
2. Pour ½ cup of water in your pot, then place trivet. Place ramekins in pot.
3. Close your lid, press the 'Pressure Cook' button and set your Instant Pot Mini to HIGH pressure. Allow to cook for about 10 minutes.
4. When the timer ends, do a quick release by carefully switching the pressure valve from 'sealed' to 'venting.' This will allow your Instant Pot Mini to release the trapped pressure that is holding the cooker shut.

Tip: Be extremely careful as you do this as the Instant Pot Mini will be hot, and the steam released can also burn your hands.

5. Consider using an oven mitten or pot holder.
6. Cautiously open then remove cakes, flipping them out of the ramekin onto a plate
7. Add your favorite ice cream and enjoy.

Nutritional (Per Serving):
Calories: 168
Fat: 9 g
Carbs: 7 g
Protein: 9 g

69. Vanilla Bean Cheesecake

Serves: 8
Prep Time: 15 Minutes
Cook Time: 20 Minutes
Cooling & Chilling Time: 1 Hour 40 Minutes
Release Mode: Natural
Release Time: 20 Minutes

Ingredients
- 16 oz. Cream cheese
- 2 large, organic Eggs
- 1 medium scraped Vanilla bean
- 1 tsp. Vanilla extract
- ¼ cup Stevia
- ¼ cup Raspberry chia jam

Directions
1. Add your stevia, vanilla extract, vanilla bean seeds, eggs, and cream cheese to your blender, and pulse until fully combined and smooth.
2. Carefully scoop out your mixture into a springform pan (preferably 6 inches or smaller as the larger tins will not be able to hold in the Instant Pot Mini).
3. Cover your pan with aluminum foil and set aside while you prepare your instant cooker.
4. Pour 2 cups of water into your Instant Pot Mini then fit your steamer insert just above the water. Place your springform pan in your steamer insert.

5. Cover your Instant Pot Mini and set the pressure valve to 'sealing.'
6. Set to cook by pressing the 'Pressure Cook' button and setting on HIGH pressure for about 20 minutes.
7. When the timer goes off, allow to naturally cool down for about 20 minutes before attempting to open. Carefully open and transfer your springform pan to a cool surface.
8. Allow to cool to room temperature (for about 40 minutes), top evenly with raspberry chia jam, then chill for at least an hour before serving. Enjoy!

Nutrition (Per Serving)
Calories: 280
Fat:16 g
Carbs:29 g
Protein: 3 g

70. Instant Pot Mini Molten Lava Cake

Serves: 3
Prep Time: 5 Minutes
Cook Time: 15 Minutes
Release Mode: Quick
Release Time: 10 Minutes

Ingredients
- 1 egg
- 2 tbsp., extra virgin Olive oil
- 2 tbsp. Stevia
- 4 tbsp., whole Milk
- 4 tbsp. Almond flour
- 1 tbsp. Cacao powder
- ½ tsp. Salt
- ½ tsp, Xanthan gum

Directions
1. Prepare ramekins by lightly greasing them with oil and setting aside.
2. Pour a cup of water into your Instant Pot Mini and fit a trivet inside the pot.
3. Combine all your ingredients in a medium bowl and mix well. Pour your batter evenly into your greased ramekins so that they are ¾ way full.

4. Carefully place your ramekins into your Instant Pot Mini on the trivet. Cover your Instant Pot Mini and set the pressure valve to 'sealing.'
5. Set to cook on the 'pressure' mode by pressing the 'Pressure Cook button with LOW pressure for about 6 minutes.
6. When the timer goes off perform a quick release, by pressing 'cancel' then carefully turning the pressure valve to venting.
Tip: Consider using a pot holder, or long spoon to turn the valve as it will be extremely hot.
7. Carefully open and remove the ramekins from the Instant Pot Mini.
8. Top lightly with powdered stevia, serve, and enjoy!

Nutrition (Per Serving)
Calories: 150
Fat:7 g
Carbs:15 g
Protein: 5 g

Conclusion

You did it! Congrats on getting all the way to the end of the Complete Ketogenic Instant Pot Mini Cookbook for Beginners: Quick, Healthy, and Foolproof Instant Pot Recipes for Rapid Weight Loss and Saving Time using 3-Quart Models! This was indeed your very first hurdle to becoming a master of the Instant Pot Mini, and the first of many positive hurdles to come.

I hope you have enjoyed all the IP Mini recipes, and that you will continue to enjoy them along your entire Ketogenic journey.

What happens next?

The next step is to continue practicing and enjoying the recipes as you see fit. Then when you are ready to begin another adventure join me again on yet another one of my amazing culinary journeys.

Join my newsletter at http://cosmicrecipes.com where you'll receive free updates and resources from me.

You'll also receive a 10-Recipe Sampler "Taste of Instant Pot Cooking" which highlighted my favourite 10 home-made recipes!

Remember to leave me a positive review if you liked what you read.

Until next time, keep on cooking. Best of luck!

About the Author

Sarah Orwell is a health and personal development coach who has helped many individuals, just like you, to lose weight and reclaim their health, well-being, and happiness.

She has a son and a daughter and she currently resides in Mount Carmel in sunny Israel.

Her life mission was revealed when she met and helped a middle-aged man completely turn his life around. Little did she know that this man is her soon-to-be fiancé.
Christopher H. went from being thirty pounds overweight to a slimmer, healthier, and confident person once again.

Sarah truly believed that Christopher meeting her was no coincidence and this intersection has kickstarted Sarah's lifelong mission of wanting to impact thousands of other people to lose weight through healthy recipes, exercises, and Personal Development Resources.

Today, Sarah works with people from all walks of life, and she has embarked on her journey to create a website filled with delicious and mouth-watering recipes that everyone can use to cook for themselves!

Check her newly-created website at cosmicrecipes.com

Index

1

14-Day Meal Plan, 22

A

Arroz Con Pollo, 72
Asparagus, 60, 146
Avocado oil, 27

B

bacon, 58, 59, 73, 125, 126
Bacon, 72
Balsamic Chicken, 108
Beef Brisket Pho, 143
Beef Curry Stew, 152
Beef flank steak, 70
Beef Pot Roast, 22, 23, 24, 78
Beef Short Ribs, 110
bell peppers, 35
Bone Broth, 154
Broccoli Cheese Soup, 158
Brussel sprouts, 16, 58
Brussels Sprouts, 58
Buffalo Ranch Chicken with Dip, 22, 23, 24, 54
Buttons of the Instant Pot Mini, 10

C

Cabbage Soup, 122
Carnitas Lettuce Wraps, 22, 23, 24, 38
cauliflower rice, 45, 72, 73
Cauliflower Soup, 124
cheddar cheese, 25, 54, 55, 124, 125, 158, 159
chicken carcass, 154
Chicken Chili Verde, 133

Chicken Curry, 22, 23, 24, 74
Chicken Faux Pho, 139
Chicken Soup with Kale, 141
Chicken thighs, 72
Chicken Tikka Masala, 94
Chickpea Soup, 129
Chili, 42, 47, 118, 127, 133, 156
chives, 25, 53
Combination Pressure Release, 13
Cottage Cheese, 64
Creamy Salsa Chicken, 116
Curried Chicken with Cauliflower, 22, 23, 24, 66

D

Dairy Free Beef Stroganoff, 88

E

Egg, 92, 164
eggs, 25, 27, 28, 29, 33, 160, 162
Eggs, 16, 27, 29, 32, 160, 162
Erythritol, 68

F

Foods You Can Eat on a Ketogenic Diet, 16

G

Goulash Soup, 120
Green Curry Cauliflower & Broccoli, 80

H

Holiday Chicken in An Instant Pot Mini, 96

J

Jerk Pork Roast, 98

K

Keto Chocolate Mini Cakes, 22, 23, 24, 160

L

Lamb Stew, 135
Loaded Cauliflower Soup, 124
Low Carb Bone Broth, 154

M

Mexican Beef, 104
Mexican Meatloaf, 90
milk, 11, 25, 30, 31, 64, 65, 66, 67, 74, 124, 125, 138, 152, 153
Molten Lava Cake, 22, 23, 24, 164

N

Natural Pressure Release, 13
No Noodle Lasagna, 92

O

olive oil, 34, 42, 45, 73, 90, 108, 111, 131
onion, 39, 46, 57, 73, 83, 84, 85, 87, 90, 92, 99, 101, 102, 104, 111, 113, 123, 125, 126, 131, 132, 133, 134, 141, 143, 145, 146, 149, 154, 157, 159
Onion Soup, 150
oregano, 39, 48, 49, 72, 86, 87, 118, 141, 142, 148, 149

P

pork, 16, 39, 45, 48, 49, 83, 84, 85, 99, 101, 102, 103, 106, 107, 113, 114, 127, 128, 148, 149, 150, 157
Pork and Kraut, 82
Pork Cheek Stew, 148
Pork Chops, 106, 114
Pork Ribs, 68
Pork Roast & Gravy, 112
Pork Roast with Mushroom Gravy, 84

Pressure Release Methods, 13
Prosciutto, 60
Prosciutto-wrapped Asparagus, 60
Pulled Pork Chili, 127

Q

Quiche, 22, 23, 24, 25
Quick Pressure, 13

R

Rice Milk Porridge, 22, 23, 24, 30
Ropa Vieja, 70

S

sausage, 27, 132
Sausage, 27, 131
Scotch Eggs, 22, 23, 24, 27
Shredded Chicken, 76
Smokey Barbecue Beans, 22, 23, 24, 56
Spare Ribs, 102
Spicy Brazilian Fish Stew, 137
spinach, 16
Split Asparagus Soup, 146
Steamed Artichokes, 62
Stewed Chicken, 86
Stewed Pork, 100

T

Tomatillo Chili, 156

V

Vanilla Bean Cheesecake, 22, 23, 24, 162

W

Whole Chicken, 96

Z

Zuppa Toscana, 131

CPSIA information can be obtained
at www.ICGtesting.com
Printed in the USA
LVHW05s0002141018
593401LV00001B/1/P